TRANS-HIMALAYAN TRADE
A RETROSPECT
(1774-1914)
(In Quest of Tibet's Identity)

Trans-Himalayan Trade
A Retrospect
(1774-1914)
(IN QUEST OF TIBET'S IDENTITY)

Phanindra Nath Chakrabarti

CLASSICS INDIA PUBLICATIONS
DELHI   **INDIA**

Published by:

CLASSICS INDIA PUBLICATIONS
JU—69B, Peetam Pura
Delhi—110034 (INDIA)

First Edition, 1990

Price Rs. 120

ISBN 81—85132—10—0

Printed at:
Amar Composing Agency, Delhi-32

DEDICATED

TO THE SACRED MEMORY OF MY
FATHER LATE PRAMATHA NATH
CHAKRABARTI OF NATOR

Contents

Part III
Decline of Commerce

Glossary

Amban	Chinese political representative or Chinese Resident officials at Lhasa in Tibet.
Dalai	A Mongolian word, meaning ocean of wisdom
Ganden	A monastery founded by Tsong Khapa, meaning place of joy.
Gossain	The celebrated Indian traders in Tibet enjoyed complete freedom in trade in Tibet. Originally resident of Kashmir mostly passed their lives in Tibet and took very important part in India-Tibet political relations.
Horsok	Actually Hor and Sok, the two distinct races, while the formers are Turks and the later are Mongol race.
Kalmukhs	Originally Russian traders later established themselves in China.
JASB	Journal of Asiatic Society of Bengal
JBORS	Journal of Bihar and Orissa Research Society

INTRODUCTION

Though the connection between India and Tibet, her Hima-layan neighbour, is very old we have not adequately paid heed to the strategical importance of this region until the Chinese invasion of Tibet in 1950 and the Sino-Indian confrontation in 1962 took place which gave us a rudest shock to India's complacency. For the first time in the history of India-China relation the act of spilling blood took place in the rough, useless Himalayan tract breaking the long silence and making the region restive. As a result, the Indian sentiment, in general, was hurt heavily.

Again, hardly was the ink of the India-China agreement of 29 April, 1954, for mutual trade between the 'Tibet Region of China' and India expressing the belief that India-China rela-tions over the common border could be maintained with 'mutual respect for each other's territorial integrity and sove-reignty, mutual non-aggression, mutual non-interference in each other's internal affairs, equality and mutual benefit and peaceful co-existence', dry, a new chapter of betrayal in the history of mutual relations opened up.

China had long been striving to exert her political control over Tibet creating deep-seated source of friction as well as a running sore poisoning Sino-Tibet relations. But this was less known to the outer world because of statements issued from time to time by the Tibetan hierarchy mentioning Tibet as a subject state of China. To explain this riddle we would have to throw light on contemporary British policy in India which was obviously aggrasive one and Tibet's fear for British military intervention into her region was not at all baseless though on the part of the British power in India of the time, it was not really possible for them to intervene in Tibetan affairs. This has been discussed and explained in the relevant chapter of this book. Any way, while collusive design of China was exacerbating her relation with Tibet, the English East India company authorities in India like Cornwallis desisted to handle Tibetan affairs and remained aloof in matters of Chinese entry into Tibet and later her attempt to intervene into Tibet's internal affairs.

The cost of this British policy had to pay by India heavily in 1950s.

Hesitant Indian initiatives, when the hermit kingdom of Tibet was invaded, turned this sleepy table land into a cockpit of international rivalry. As a consequence, Tibet formed a fiercely controversial zone of conflicting interests. A question may arise why should India not take up the policy of squatting on the fence while it was not possible on her part to help Tibet in her plight.

This developed in me the interest to know the reasons of unfriendly and aggressive attitude of China towards India. To follow-up the reasons I am to hunt every leaf of East India Company's historical documents during its formative years when the Company began extending its politico-economic relation with, Tibet.

I have also tried to examine the qualitative development, method, approach, interactions and reasons of Company's attempts at establishing commercial relations with Tibet. Economically undeveloped Tibet drew the attention of the Company and the latter sincerely tried to develop commercial relation with her————the reason was not a simple one but a combination of necessities felt by the Company.

In the book I have also tried to throw sufficient light on the politico-economic relations of Tibet with India under British rule and China under imperial dynasty, anatomising the political identity of Tibet and the fallacy maintained by China that Tibet was her vassal state. Writing on this aspect is somewhat a difficult task because of non-availability of Tibetan and Chinese documents and this has become more difficult by the statements issued from time to time by the Tibetan hierarchy mentioning Tibet as a subject state of China only to keep the English in India away from their country.

Initially, the English East India Company authorities announced their desire to establish a commercial relation with Tibet but a close review of the activities of all the British Commercial Missions would show, that not a single mission was sent aiming at establishing commercial contact with Tibet. The ultimate aim of the English was to obtain permission from the Tibetan authorities for allowing the English merchants to go to China through Tibet for commerce. There is actually no reason to believe that the English Company in India had a mind to carry on trading activities with Tibet for, the volume of trade with her was not at all encouraging. The Tibetan merchants dealt chiefly in tea, some of them to the extent of two or three lakhs of rupees a year of the then value of £ 20,000 to £ 30,000. It is equally difficult to believe that the English East India Company, so far one of the best mercantile organisations in the world of the time, would undertake such a foolish venture which would cost them men, money and labour in return of an insignificant volume of trade.

A number of standard works based on deep research, have been written on different aspects of Tibet, Nepal, Bhutan and Sikkim but a survey of politico-economic relation of Tibet with both of her giant neighbours, India and China, is remarkably absent. In this book I have tried to throw some light on this aspect. However, mention of name of some scholars engaged in writing on these tiny Himalayan states may be of some interests. Sir Charles Bell (*Tibet Past and Present*, 1924) ; R.S. Gundry (*China ond her Neighbours*, 1893) ; Arthur W. Humel (*Eminent Chinese of the Ch'ing Period*, 2 Vols, 1943-44), containing much useful informations on China's contact with Tibet, W.W. Rockhill (*The Dalai Lama of Lhasa and their Relations with Manchu Emperors of China 1644-1908, 1910*),

A. Lamb (*Britain and Chinese Central Asia, The Road to Lhasa, 1767—1905*, 1960); S.Cammann, (*Trade through the Himalayas, the Early British attempt to open Tibet*, 1951) ; C. Wessels (*Early Jesuit Travellers in Central Asia*); Jahar Sen, (*Indo-Nepal Trade ; in the Nineteenth Century, 1977*), P.K. Jha (*History of Sikkim, 1817—1904*, 1985) A.B. Majumdar (*Britain and the Himalayan kingdom of Bhotan*, 1984).

In fact, no work has yet been contributed to the economic history of Tibet during the period of our discussion by any scholar. Therefore, the picture of Tibetan trade and commerce remains unknown, and makes any writing on this aspect hard because of non-availability of source material. The data problems have been overcome and then defficiencies apply a *fortiori* to the chronicle data-poor medieval Tibet. Again all materials for this book have been collected mostly from the records of the English East India Company. Hence there is no possibility here of conducting a rigorous quantitative analysis.

Analysing the politico-economic relations between China and Tibet, I have tried to examine the unilateral demand of China on Tibet.

The present book is actually an enlarged version of an article originally presented to the XXXII ICANAS held in Hamburg, W. Germany in 1986.

I could not, however, treat the whole Eastern and Northern region of the Himalayas in this book. The Northern region, I hope, would be treated in the next volume.

ACKNOWLEDGEMENT

My debt to Professor Jagadish Narayan Sarkar, ex-head, Department of History, Jadavpur University, under whose feet I learnt method of research in history, is too deep for wards. I also acknowledge my humble gratitude to Professor D.P. Sinha, ex-head, Department of History, North Bengal University. I have to sincerely thank Dr. Kanai Lal Chattopadhaya without whose active help my project could not have seen the light of day. My thanks are due to Dr. Malay Sankar Bhattacharyya, Secretary, Indian Institute of Oriental Studies and Research, Calcutta, who imbibed in me a passion for writing on this aspect while Dr. Gautam Neogi, my friend, helped me with books needed by me.

India Office Library, London, and its staff are entitled to my sincere thanks for the generous help they rendered to me during my study there.

Lastly, my thanks are due to Srimati Anima Chakrabarti, my wife, who has encouraged me all along. Dr. Shyamal Banerjee and his beautiful wife Srimati Poly Banerjee, M. Sc., of Manchester, U.K. are to be given my regards for the help they extended me during my stay in U.K. I am most greatful to Dr. Sunit Ghatak, the medical practitioner in London, for his sincerity and friendship.

I have received unfailing co-operations from my friend Prof. Dr. Ranjit Sen, M.A.. Ph. D., D. Litt., for which I shall always remain greatful to him.

I must register my sincere thanks to my friend Dr. Arun kr. Sil, a medical scientist, National award holder on Tuberculosis Research, 1970, Founder of Boy Scout of Bengal and Pioneer Scouts of India, who spent his valuable time in throwing new light on the topic during our long discussion.

Sri Praveen Sareen, the owner of Classics India Publications is entitled to my sincere thanks in undertaking the publication of the work.

Dewali   P.N. Chakrabarti
Calcutta-700031

CHAPTER I

I

THE LAND AND THE PEOPLE

To most of our countrymen, Tibet was a mysterious, secluded country in the remote hinterland of the Himalayas about which we have come to learn from the explorers and travellers that it is a forbidden land though it is contiguous for nearly a thousand miles with India, from Kashmir to Burma. Despite our inadequate knowledge about Tibet and her people there was always some kind of intercourse between India and her. But we have never tried to acquire knowledge about the land and her people who eke out a precarious living there.

From the great central range of the peaks of the Himalayas on the eastern side, to the Indo-Gangetic plains it covers an area where slopes are found into alternate ravines and ridges deeply eroded by flowing water and gradually sink down into the valleys of the Ganges and the Brahmaputra. On the western side, the last inhabited valleys on the Indian side of the frontier with Tibet lie enmeshed in the great tangle of mountains, the highest in the world, known as the Western Himalayas. It stretches from the vicinity of Upper Nepal in the East to an area much further north where Kashmir meets China and Afghanistan and the principal ranges of which lie East to West with a northward sweep as they approach Kashmir. The ranges enclosing a number of valleys are pierced by a number of passes of varying fame and much notoriety since there is not one among them which does not frequently claim the lives of travellers.

This vast area on the borders, inhabited by different classes of people having varied customs and cultures participated directly in commercial activities from very olden times since commercial operation was their life line due to extreme scarcity of agricultural field.

The Tibetans have no ethnological similarity with the Chinese. They are a Central Asian tribe having ethnic affinity extending through Mongolia to trans-Baikal peoples such as Evenks, Yakuts, Orochhins and the Tungus. In their physical characteristics, two groups of Tibetans have been distinguished : (1) a round-headed group found mostly in the cultivated river valleys of central and western Tibet, who resemble the Burmese and (2) a long-headed group who tend to be tall and angular in build with acquiline noses, found among the noble families in Central Tibet and generally among the nomads of East and North East.[1]

India and China both countries tried to create their respective influence on Tibet from very olden times. While India's attempt was limited within the spreading of her religio-cultural influences, China did this with military expedition. The Tibetans drew their religion from India. From very ancient time they have been accustomed to visit the sacred shrines of India. Tibetan traders came down to Bengal and other parts of India. Indian traders went to Tibet. Inter-marriages between the border peoples had taken place. Tibet had never been really isolated from India. Hindu pilgrims cherished the desire of visiting the sacred mountain-Kailash atleast once in their life time.

The Himalayan system is composed of three great culminating chains running more or less parallel to each other for their whole length. The inner and most northern of the three ranges is naturally divided into a Western and an Eastern sections. The Western is known as the Karakorum Range separating the valley of the Indus from the Yarkand River and other streams belonging to the inland system of Lob-nor. It has vast glaciers and lofty peaks, including that called K2 (28000 ft.). This Range is traversed by passes of great height, such as Chang-Chenmo (19,000 ft.),[2] and the Karakoram (18,000 ft.). The sources of three great rivers are on the southern slopes of the northern range, and forcing their way through the central and southern chains, they reach the plains of India : namely, the Indus, Sutlej and Brahmaputra. The Eastern section of the Northern Range forms the natural northern boundary of Greater Tibet. Further north there is an extensive region which has been taken as part of Tibet in the modern map really inhabited by wandering independent tribes, called Hor and Sok.[3] Tibet, the name most probably came from the Turks and Persians. Formerly the name Tangut[4] had been used. But the true name is 'Bod Land' where Bod or Bodyul[5] lived. Lhasa, the capital of Tibet and official residence of the Dalai Lama is located in the valley of Ki-chu, (Latitude 29.39° 17″ N and 11,700 ft. above the sea). It stands on a plain land, surrounded by mountains, and a large number of monasteries. The vast height of the fringing ranges, the bleakness of the landscape in general, and the extremes of climate have always made Tibet comparatively inaccessible to outsiders. Though the Tibetans have taken to discouraging all visitors from India fairly recently and the country has come to be called 'forbidden land', it was not so closed formerly. On the contrary, it was open to external influences through trade and other cultural and religious contacts from India.

The inhospitable physical features of Tibet which discouraged invaders but caused it to become a refuge area for peoples of various races since the dawn of history, though not all of these were refugees in the usual sense of the term.[6] Until the 7th century A.D., it was just a territory of scattered tribes, and the peoples of Tibet were unable to form a nation. The historians of T'ang Dynasty (A.D. 618-907) of China describes the Tibetans as nomadic, who practised human sacrifice.[7]

The early Tibetans practised a religion which is known as

Bon-Po, the similarity of whose lies with Shamanism practised in its purest form by the Tungus of the Amur basin. Tsong-Ka-Pa, the noted religious reformer of Tibet, created the Yellow or Gelukpa sect[8] and the Lamaism is actually the Tibetan form of Buddhism. Gradually the Lamas became heads of temporal and administrative matters.

Attached with a monastery, a Lama had several obligations. These were not only to his monastery, but also its thousands of inmates and to the many Tibetan people who lived all around, their whole existence tied up with that of the monastery and dependent on it.

The early Tibetans were a war-like people. They carried on successful wars against China upto the time of their conversion to Buddhism. King Namri Srongtsan brought about the unification of Tibet[9] and achieved such a reputation that even the Chinese feared him of his courage and for the strength and success of his armies. In the second decade of the seventh century Srongtsan Gampo or Srong-btsan-sGam – Po (b.61 7 A.D) became known as a powerful, just and profound king. He is believed to have come from Ladakh where Indian civilization flourished since the time of Harappa culture[10]. He sent sixteen Tibetan students to India to study under various great teachers both Buddhist and Hindu. One of his ministers Thoumi Sambhota was also sent to India. Here he had learned to devise Tibetan script of thirty letters, based largely on the Kashmiri *Sharada* alphabet, and on the classical *nagri* script, making changes to suit the different phonetics of the Tibetan language. Then they set to work translating Hindu and Buddhist scriptures, into Tibetan. Thus the Indian religion and culture both spreaded throughout Tibet.

Srongtsan Gampo then carried on military campaigns that had become traditional to Tibetan Kings, and finding the ancestral capital in Yarlung too remote from the centre of the newly united kingdom, he moved to Lhasa and there built himself a camparatively modest fort in the top of the Red Hill, Marpori, the exact site of the future Potala. He had first married the Nepali princess Bhrikuti, who was a devout

Buddhist. Then he turned his attention to China and demanded to marry a Chinese princess. The refusal of the Chinese emperor made him angry and pushed his conquest further towards China and sacked its capital. This military might quickly persuaded the Chinese Emperor Tai Tsung to give consent to the marriage. Like Bhrikuti, the princess Wong Shen Kenjo was also a devout Buddhist.[11] Buddhism and Bon religion thus managed to live side by side and the former was confined largely to the Royal Family.

After the death of Srongtsan Gampo, his successors continued further the military campaign, defeated China and forced her to pay tribute to Tibet. It is interesting here to mention that all the military campaigns of Tibetan kings were directed to China not to India. The reason is not difficult to find. Tibet looked to India for spiritual and intellectual guidance whereas with China she maintained a relation of rivalry since time immemorial. Buddhism had already divided into two schools of thought—Theg Man or Hinayana and Theg Chen or Mahayana school. Later the tantricism came to Tibet from India and gave Tibetan Buddhism its particular shape combining with the original Bon beliefs. Lopon Rimpoche, the famous Tantric monk, earned an extraordinary reputation, and was believed to have been born from a lotus. In India he was known as *Padmasambhava*. It seems that he was born in that part of the country which lies between Kashmir and Afghanistan, a region corresponding roughly to the modern Swat. But with the death of Lopon Rimpoche, Chinese religious influence began to grow in strength in Tibet. Subsequently, faced with stiff resistance from Indian doctrine all Chinese hopes of founding religious influence in Tibet were lost. By decree the Indian school of thought, known as the Nagarjuna School, became the only lawful form of Buddhism in Tibet. All Chinese monks had to leave Tibet.

By the time Atish Dipankara Srijnana, the great Indian scholar, who came to propagate Buddhism in Tibet, died in the middle of the eleventh century A.D., the monasteries were fast assuming political importance. There was no central king in Tibet and the country was divided amongst rival petty chiefs.

It was Kublai Khan, the Mongol Emperor of China, made Phakpa[12] as the central political ruler of Tibet subduing effectively the vestiges of power among the Tibetan chiefs. He brought about the unification of the country destroying the petty chiefs and placed the country under a joint political and religious leadership. He built up a central administrative machinery giving the people law and justice. Trade and financial activities developed. The whole country was divided into thirteen provinces, each governed by an administrator selected from the best candidates.

After Phakpa, disintegrating forces crept in due to weak successors. The country needed a strong ruler having spiritual force. Such a need was fulfilled in the person of Tsong Khapa, who was born in Amdo province, of a nomad couple. Under him Buddhist monasteries rose in prominence and extended their influence far beyond the monastery walls. Tsong Khapa founded his own monastery, known as *Ganden* meaning Place of Joy (in the sense of perfection). His followers came to be known as *Gelukpa* sect.

Tsong Khapa was succeeded first by Gyal Tsats and then by Khadrub who died around the year 1475. Most probably, it was at this time theory of incarnation was introduced[13]. Sonam Gyatso, the incarnation, quickly extended his reputation which allured Altan Khan, the Mongolian ruler, to invite him in his court. At this time the Ming dynasty in China was becoming weaker and the Mongol armies continued invasions into China. The Mongols also posed a great threat to Tibet. But Sonam Gyatso made it possible to spread Buddhism throughout the length and breadth of Mongolia inducing Altan Khan to embrace Buddhism who proclaimed it as the national religion of Mongolia thenceforth. The Khan bestowed on Sonam Gyatso the title of Dalai Lama. Dalai, a Mongolian word, means wisdom and Gyatso, in Tibetan, meaning ocean. The Dalai Lama therefore, means Ocean of Wisdom. Visiting Altan Khan's court in Mongolia, Gyatso went to the imperial court of China on his way back.

The fifth Gyalwa Rimpoche (1617-82) or Dalai Lama[14] was far and near renowned for his military expedition and political astuteness. It was during this period Chinese manoeuvres set in for the imposition of their colonial regime firmly in Tibet but foiled by Gyalwa Rimpoche. He successfully established Tibet's absolute independence and sovereignty.

From Fr. Desideri's account we come to learn that the struggle for power between two high Rimpoche of the Gelukpa sect, Gyalwa Rimpoche and the Panchen Rimpoche had begun from this time and the Chinese began exploiting the situation to split the country. But the attempt was baffled[15]. The Seventh Dalai Lama (1708-58) was chosen by the Tibetans themselves. He was not interested in temporal matter which was taken over by Panchen Rimpoche. Backed by the Chinese *Ambans*, stationed in Lhasa, Panchen played the role of a puppet in the hands of the Chinese. The pattern was set for the Chinese to follow down to the present day.

Most probably, it was Gyalwa Rimpoche, the Fifth Dalai Lama, who introduced the system of granting land farms to Panchen Rimpoche near Shigtase, where the monastery of Tashilhumpo was founded. This is the reason for which Panchen is known as Tashi Lama.

Pursuading the Dalai Lama to visit the imperial court, China, however, managed to establish a connection with Tibet but she did not dare to put any political pressure on Tibet intending to impose her political authority, on the contrary, he was received with great honour and valuable gifts were given to him. This was most probably due to the fact that the Dalai Lama exercised tremendous influence on the Mongolian ruler who was a dreaded enemy of China. Entreated by the Chinese authority, the Dalai adjudicated the border dispute between Chinese and Mongolians and the latter lessened their raids on Chinese territory.[16] This was perhaps the first instance in which the Dalai Lama exercised purely political authority to mitigate dispute between two foreign independent states.

The growing friendship between the Mongolian Kings and Tibetan Lamas was not at all to the likings of the Chinese. Hard pressed by the Mongols to the north and the dormant fighting zeal and skill of the Tibetans to their west, the Chinese could not take any action, political or military, against Tibet except attempting to manipulate the succession of the Dalai to their political ends. This continued uptil 1788 when Nepal invaded Tibet and in the trail of which Chinese army, being requested by the then Dalai, entered into Tibet and drove the Gurkhas out of the country which we would discuss latter on.

They were now in a better position to exert more direct political control over Tibet. Two political representatives, better known as *Ambans* and 'an army were permanently posted in Lhasa. Backed by the force of the army the *Ambans* began supervising the selections of each succeeding incarnation of the Dalai Lama. They closed Tibet to the outer world. They did also what they could to subvert the position of the Dalai Lama by supporting and encouraging Panchen against him.[17]

REFERENCES

1. The Encyclopaedia Britannica, vol. 1 (15th ed.), Lond. 1935 p. 757.

2. The two passes namely Pangtungla, 18,900 ft. high and Changlung-barma-la, 19, 280 ft.

3. *Horsok* is the name given by the Tibetans to the whole region between the Northern Himalayan Range (Nyench-hen-Thangla) and the Kuen-lun. It is inhabited by two distinct races, called Hor and Sok. Harpa is the western half of this region, Sokpa, the eastern half, as well as part of Sokeul, round the Kokonor Lake. They are all styled Khachhen (Muhammadans) by the Tibetans. Sokyeul is the same as Tangut. The Hor are Turks, and the Sok are of Mongol race. Yeul means an encampment, so that Sokyeul is the encampment of the Soks or Mongols.

4. The origin of which has been explained by Col. Yule in his *Marco-Polo*, Vol, i, P. 209 (India Office Library, London).

5. In India the land was called Bhotiya and inhabitants were Bhot. J.O. Thomson, *History of Ancient Geography*, Cambridge 1948 (I.O.L, London).

6. S.W. Bushell, *The Early History of Tibet from Chinese sources*, J.R.A.S., Vol. XII (Lond. 1880), pp. 435-541.

7. *Ibid.*

8. The essential difference between the 'Yellow hat' and 'Red hat' is that the Red follows the old translation of Buddhism while the yellow believes in later translation. Before Tsong Khapa it was the custom for all monks to wear red hats. Later the breakaway monks from old translation school began wearing yellow hat with a view to introducing them as separate entity. Yellow colour in Tibet is known as purity and growth and Red is associated with physical strength and power or authority. Black represents force of warfare and white is peace. The monks embraced Gelukpa sect and wear yellow hat does not necessarily mean that he is not authorised to wear Red hat, on the contrary, he can easily put on it for some reasons he thinks it will benefit his progress.

   Ippolito Desideri. Fillippo De-Felippi (ed), *An Account of Tibet*, pp. 30-32, Lond, 1932 (I.O.L. London). Desideri, the Jesuit father, came to Tibet in 1716 for the propagation of Christianity and returned to Nepal in 1727.

9. His name is spelled in Tibetan Srong—btsan SGam—po, but in rendering this and other Tibetan names, we are giving the phonetic simplifications, omitting the letters usually not pronounced.

10. Rev. A.H. Francke, *The kingdom of GNYA—Khribtsampo, the first king of Tibet*, Journal and Proceedings of the Asiatic Society of Bengal (Cal. 1910), P. 99.

11. *Ibid.* Rockhill, *Life of the Buddha* (Lond. 1844), p. 213 C.P. Fitzerald, *China, A short Cultural History* (N. York and Lond. 1938).

12. Around the 1071 Koncho Gyepo founded Sakya Monastery, so called, because it was built on a site where the earth was coloured grey (Sa-Kya). Kancho Gyepo's grandson was Kunga Gyaltson, also known as Sakya Pandita, or the Sakya Grand Lama. His nephew was Phakpa.

13. In Tibet nearly every monastery is the place of such an incarnate Lama often descended from the original founder of the monastery.

14. Dalai Lama is the highest but by no means the only incarnate Changchub Sempa or *bodhisttva*, which is an ideal, the highest

goal for a monk is to achieve his own liberation only to renounce it and to return for the benefit of others. He is the head of the Gelukpa sect, but he is also spiritual and temporal head of the whole of Tibet and is accej ted unanimously by all sects. Thubten Jigme Norbu and Collin Turnbull, *Tibet*, Middlesex, U.K. 1969, p. 220.

15. Desideri, op. cit. pp. 317-18.

   Jesuit Fr. Ippodito Desideri came to Tibet in the first decade of 18th century for the propagation of Chriastainity and returned to Nepal in 1727. He was made particularly welcome to Tibet because of his great scholarship and his willingness to study under Tibetan teachers. He was given every freedom by the Regent who was then ruling Tibet. At Sera monastery he was given his own private rooms and allowed to use one as a chapel Christian Worship. He learnt Tibetan language and scripture and translated several important Tibetan scriptures.

16. Following books were also consulted for this information. S.W. Bushel, *The Early History of Tibet from Chinese sources* : A.H. Francke, *The kingdom of GNYA—Khri—btsampo, the first king of Tibet*.

17. Peoples of Tibet were not divided into classes, but Lhasa was an exception. In Lhasa, |the] highest ranking peoples were the high monastery officials such as the abbots, then the monks and government officials who form a kind of lay nobility. Then came the mule suppliers and traders, the merchant class, and then a number of specialist workers such as printers, weavers, cooks, carpenters, potters, stone and wood carvers, gold and silver smiths, the black smiths, the butchers and the disposers of the dead were regarded with contempt.

II

A SURVEY OF
INDO-TIBETAN TRADE AND COMMERCE

Since time immemorial India carried on intra-Asian overland trade with her Himalayan neighbours. Kautilya's *Arthasastra* mentions that the beginning of India's trade-link with Tibet can be traced five hundred years before the Christian era began. A number of countries such as Bhutan, Sikkim, Nepal, Kashmir, Tibet, China and Central Asia beyond the Himalayas, maintained close commercial link with India though direct link with Tibet since 1949 had been cut off due to political reasons.

Geographically, these countries are linked together with one another by chains of snow-clad mountain system covering a distance of hundreds of miles. Both the Indian and Tibetan merchants visited their respective lands with their indigenous products. The first Indian adventurers to Tibet, however, were the religious minded people ; the second were the merchants. The Pundits (title conferred on some Indian merchants) had the ability of surveying the tracts of the Himalayas. Kashyap Matunga, the first Indian monk had gone to China crossing Tibet for preaching religion (lst Century A.D.).

This age-old and traditional trade came to be stopped when the English East India Company desired to penetrate into this trade with the obvious object to reach China through

Tibet.   Here we would like to throw some light on the econo-
mic condition and commercial prospect of Tibet   when   British
East India Company attempted   at   economic penetration into
Tibet.

(a)   First Europeans in Tibet

A.M. Davies, the biographer of Warren Hastings, the first
Governor General of India, lamented that even in the mideigh-
teenth century Tibet was 'a land of mystery.........which was
not only unknown to the West, but had hitherto been closed to
all contact with the West'.[1]

But the statement seems to be wrong. In fact, long before
the period mentioned above, Ralph Fitch, an English merchant-
adventurer, arrived at Coochbehar[2] in 1584 in order to survey
the real position of trade between Bengal and Tibet.[3] Even
before Fitch, as far back as the 14th century, Father Odoric of
Pordenone went to Lhasa, though Berthhold Laufer has,
however, disproved this legend in his book '*Was Odoric of
Pordenone ever in Tibet*'[4].

However, according to evidence, Antonio Andrade and
Manuel Marquis, the two Portuguese Jesuits, went to Tibet in
1624 and founded a Christian mission at Tsaparang in Western
Tibet.[5] Shortly after, two more Portuguese Jesuits, Father
Cabral and Father Cacella visited Shigatse in Central Tibet.
But the hostility of the Lamas prevented them from founding
a mission there[6].   None of those missions could reach Lhasa.
The first European who went to Lhasa was a famous monk
named Father Gruber. He set out for Lhasa in 1661 with
Father d' Orville, his companion, through China and even-
tually came to India.   They reached Lhasa on October 8. 1661.
The interesting account he had left behind is novel in many
ways[7].

Then in the first half of the 18th century, the Capuchins
had a mission in Lhasa itself[8].   The Jesuit Father Desideri,
an European monk, had gone to Lhasa *via* Nepal in 1716 and
lived there for a couple years and subsequently coming back
to Nepal in December 1727 wrote an excellent book giving his
remarkable impression on Tibet[9].

Facts, therefore, establish that at least from 17th century onwards, Europe maintained contact with Tibet. A number of European religious preachers visited Tibet with the obvious intention of baptizing the local people into Christianity. Nobody except Ralph Fitch, surveyed the commercial potentiality of Tibet upto that period. Fitch sailed with the Queen's letter from London abroad the *Tiger* for India on 13th February, 1583'[10] At Ormuz he was imprisoned by the Portuguese and brought to Goa. Having escaped therefrom Fitch arrived at Agra in 1584. 'From there he went to Fatehpur Sikri, where Akbar, the Mughal Emperor, then resided. He sought an inteview with Akbar, the great Mughal, to present his sovereign's letter.' Fitch is silent on whether the interview ever took place or not. However, from Agra he came to Bengal *via* Allahabad, Benares and Patna with a fleet of 180 boats, laden with merchandize[11]. He came to Malda and thence at Cooch Behar[12].

It is interesting to note that an ordinary merchant-traveller, like Ralph Fitch, came to Cooch Behar, taking enormous risk only to survey the commercial prospects of Tibet, particularly when the ordinary people of Europe had little or no idea about that country. It is really a mystery, how was it possible for Fitch to come to know about Tibet.

Obtaining the *Dewani* of Bengal, Bihar and Orissa in 1765, the English East India Company began to establish commercial relation with Tibet under the leadership of the first Governor General of the Company in India, Warren Hastings. His excessively keen desire to open up the commercial door of Tibet evinces the deeprooted desire of the East India Company to enter into Tibet. The primary consideration of the East India Company was trade and it was apparently known to the company about atleast one of the commercial possibilities of Tibet—its borax production since 1644[13].

English East India Company's attempt to penetrate into Tibet had an unique characteristic. The attempts were not confined among the Englishmen, the servants of the Company alone, but some Indians were also sent as and when the Company authorities felt it necessary. The most important difference between the English and Indian missions to Tibet was that while the missions headed by the English maintained diary containing their day-to-day experiences which makes them worthful to the posterity, the rock-like ignorance of the Indians, about the necessity of keeping such diaries for the future generations, have made them almost obscure explorers.

Here one strange thing should also be mentioned. Though all the initial attempts to open the door of Tibetan commerce started from Bengal, the people of Bengal are not found to be interested or aware about the events that took place around them. They neither tried to perceive the gravity of the contemporary events nor the momentous commercial prospects of Tibet.

(b) *Commodities—import and export*

It has already been mentioned at the outset that India carried on commercial activities with Tibet from very olden Times. But the transaction was one-sided only. Indian commodities had a very promising market in Tibet, though consumers were not Tibetans, whereas Tibetan goods had insignificant demand in India. The Tibetan merchants bought Indian merchandise in lieu of gold dust[14]. The buyers of Indian goods in Tibet were very many viz., the Tibetans, Chinese, Russians (Kalmukhs) and Kashmiries. Buying Indian goods, all these merchants sold them mostly to Chinese merchants who in turn sold those to the Chinese consumers. A very insignificant quantity was bought by a handful of upper class Tibetans. Naturally therefore, an indirect India-China trade was extant through Tibet since a long time.

A comparative chart of export and import to and from Tibet will reveal the volume of India's trade with that country.

(A) *Export to Tibet from Bengal*[15]:

(a) Precious woolen staples (b) hide (c) indigo (d) spices (e) tobacco (f) sugar.

(B) *From Assam :*

(a) spices (b) wood (c) munga (d) dhuties (e) coarse linen

(f) flinen (fine) (g) white cloth (inferior quality) (h) pearl (i) coral (j) crystal (k) rosary etc.

(C) *From Kashmir* :

(a) raisin (b) sugar (c) dry fruits.

(D) *Export from Tibet to India*[16].

(a) coarse woolen cloth (b) narrow serge (c) gold (d) musk (e) cowtails (f) wool (g) salt (h) tea (brought from China).

The quantum of articles were too little. From the above chart it is found that gold was brought to India from Tibet. Throughout the seventeenth century, huge quantity of gold were brought in by the merchants of India from different countries they traded with[17].

It should be mentioned here that Indian commodities purchased by the Tibetan merchants were not actually for the cconsumption of the Tibetans but they sold those to the Chinese merchants. George Bogle, who headed the first British Commercial Mission to Tibet, observed the presence of Chinese merchants there. He mentioned in his narratives 'some Chinese merchants came to Teshu Lumboo to buy lamb skins' ....Indian goods, in particular, had a very prospetive market in China. Tea-trading was essentially a monopoly of the Tibetan merchants, who brought it from China.[18].

The purchasing capacity of the general Tibetans was almost negligible and therefore, the scope of India's trade with Tibet alone was 'very limited'[19]. Both Kirk Patrick and Abdul Qadir, members of British Mission to Tibet, surveying very carefully the prospect of India's trade with Tibet, came to the conclusion that Nepal occupied far better position than Tibet in regard to trade with India[20]. Both Indian and European commodities, they observed, had a very prospective market also in Nepal. The articles like 'woolen staples of Great Britain and warm flannels of the finer sort' had tremendous demand in Nepal[21].

Hevhannes Joughayetsi, an Armenian merchant and English East India Company's agent in Nepal, arrived at Kathmandu

on April 21, 1686, prepared a ledger in which he gave a
detailed description of trade and commerce of Nepal and
finally suggested that the Company, if desired, could carry on
a profitable trade with Nepal. He has left an exhaustive list
of at least one hundred and seventy four Indian and English
items which could be sold in Nepal[22].

Here again that pertinent question arises-who were the consumers of foreign goods in Nepal ? No accurate information
is available in this connection. But it can be asserted that the
inhabitants of Nepal except the upper class of people attached
to the royal family, were not consumers, because their financial position, as far as our practical experience is concerned,
was not at all so much sound so that they could afford to
spend money buying foreign goods for their own consumption
particularly when those goods were highly expensive. There
was, therefore, very insignificant internal demand for foreign
goods in Nepal. We have information that the merchants from
Tibet and even China flocked together at the markets of Nepal
where foreign goods were sold. Besides, Nepali merchants
had free access to Tibet where they could sell their commodities to the Chinese merchants or Indian traders who traded
with China[23]. Therefore, the ultimate destination of Indian
goods was China.

Hence, despite Nepal's potentiality in trade and commerce,
the English East India Company did not want to establish
commercial relation with Nepal. On the contrary, the servants
of the Company wanted to reach China through Tibet and sell
their goods there personally because in that case the profit
would have been enormous. Therefore, the Company sought
to have permission for free access to Tibet first. And for this
reason alone, the representative of the Company, viz. Warren
Hastings, desired to send British commercial missions to Tibet.
Direct representation to the Chinese Emperor was also sought
with the ulterior object of exploiting the vast Chinese market in
favour of Britich commerce. Documents of British commercial
activities in Tibet undoubtedly reveal that the ultimate object
of the English East India Company was to establish a commer-

cial relation with China and not with Tibet. Tibet was to be used only as a spring board.

In the British foreign policy, Tibet occupied an insignificant place though strategically her position was essentially important to India. The British in India ignored her strategical position. As the British persistently attempted to enter into Chinese Commerce, the latter, on the other hand, perseveringly obilterated the separate boundary between China and Tibet. The Chinese officials repeatedly demanded that Tibet had no separate entity, but a province only of the Chinese empire. Without examining the reality of the Chinese demand the British authorities later accepted this Chinese version.

(c) *Medium of Exchange*

The progress of trade and commerce entirely depended on the monetary situation and credit system. Bimetallism was the essential feature of monetary system of Indian subcontinent during the preiod of our discussion. Monetary conditions and the movement of treasure depend on a variety of circumstances, balance of trade, levels of internal price rates of exchange, duites, treaty arrangements as well as manipulation for fiscal purposes. With both gold and silver coins circulating and each type being valued in terms of the money of account, there were both official mint-ratios and market-ratios determined by the interaction of demand and supply.

Tibet had no mint, hence, there was no money coined of its own circulated throughout the country. All financial transactions were conducted by Chinese, Tartar and Nepalese coins. The Indian merchants, in particular, did not accept any of the above coins ; hence Indian goods were sold in exchange of gold dust.

Before the conquest of Nepal Valley by the Gorkhas, money was coined in Nepal by all royal dynasties of Kathmandu, Bhatgaon and Paton.[24] If the coins of Kathmandu rajas were marked by a sword, the coins of Bhatgaon and Paton were marked by shell and trishul (trident) respectively. But after the conquest of Nepal the Gorkhas found a stiff resistance when they tried to circulate their own money in Tibet. Hence, old money of Nepal prevailed in Tibet, financial transactions were carried on by that one[25].

But the Indian merchants who carried on trade with Tibet were reluctant to accept Nepalese money circulated in Tibet, on the contrary, they demanded gold in exchange of their merchandize. Tibetan goods, we have seen, had no demand in India and the balance of payment was in favour of her. Throughout the medieval period, Indian merchants sold their goods to foreign countries in lieu of gold and a certain portion of it must have been re-invested. But it is difficult to come to any conclusion due to paucity of direct reference. W.H. Moreland, R.C. Dutta, R.K. Mukherjee, Jagadish N. Sarkar, Tapan Ray Chaudhury, N.K. Chaudhuri, Irfan Habib, Surendra Gopal have thrown light, from time to time, on the economic activities of the Indians but the subject of re-investment have been left untouched.

(d) *Indian merchants in Tibet* :

Two classes of Indian merchants, in fact, engaged themselves as carrying agencies of trade and commerce with Tibet : (a) Kashmeries and (b) the Gossain pilgrim merchants.

George Bogle, the first Englishman, headed the British Commercial Mission to Tibet sent by Hastings, described the Kashmiries, in his chronicles, as the 'jews of Europe'[26]. Lhasa was their principal trading centre where they lived and traded. 'No duties levied on goods and trade' and they were 'protected and free from exactions'. Besides Lhasa, other places like Giantse, Shigatse and Tashilhumpo had their commercial centres[27].

There was most probably, no restriction for the ingress of the Indian merchants to Tibet. Right to entrance of the Indians other than merchants and pilgrims was, however, restricted. But the arrival of the English in Bengal and the extension of their territorial sovereignty towards northern Bengal definitely alarmed Bhutan, Nepal as well as Tibet and suspicion grew among them not only about the English but also about the subjects of the British. Even before Bogle had reached the capital of Bhutan, a messenger arrived with a letter from the Tashi Lama, better known as Panchen Lama of Tibet to Bogle. In that letter, the Lama apprised Bogle that 'no Mughal, Indian, Pathan or Englishman should be admitted to Tibet'[28]. It appears that right to admission of the Indians to Tibet was also withdrawn and that was definitely due to the presence of the English in Bengal.

Again, the influences of Indian merchants, lived in Tibet since long, on Panchen Lama was equally great. As Bogle was threatened not to enter into Tibet and the King of Bhutan declined to intercede on his behalf, Bogle put all his reliance on Purangir Gossin[29], who had arranged Bogle's journey to Tibet and was honour bound to help achieve its success. Bogle, however, narrated that Purangir was 'heavily bribed by him and only after which the latter consented to go to Panchen Lama in person to urge him to allow Bogle to enter into Tibet[30].

Now, it is not possible to know how far Bogle's verison is true. But one thing appears to be correct that without Purangir's help Bogle could not enter into Tibet and the permission obtained by Purangir for Bogle reveals the close relation between Panchen Lama and Purangir. Now let us turn our attention first to the Kashmiri merchants.

Bogle describes them as 'Armenians in the Turkish empire ; because of their far-flung commercial enterprises throughout the Eastern Kingdoms of Asia. The Kashmiris acted not only as middlemen in the China trade with Tibet but they had stationed their agents at Coromondel, Benaras, Bengal, Kashmir and Nepal to collect merchandise from more places and sent to Lhasa mainly for China trade[31] We can assume the difficulties one had to face for sending merchandise from those places to Lhasa especially by pack animals.

From Lhasa these articles were to be transported as far as Seling in China. Bogle's observation is worth-quoting here in this connection. 'The most considerable branch of commerce is with China. It is carried on by the natives of that Kingdom (Tibet), by Kashmiries, and by the Lamas' agents, who proceed to Seling, and sometimes even to Peking'[32]. Since Bogle was an an eye-witness, therefore, we cannot ignore his observation. He has given us a detailed description of the articles imported to and exported from China which will be described later on.

The next class of merchants were the Gossain pilgrims of whom Purangir was most important. They were both Hindu pilgrims and traders. *Manas Sarovar* (Lake) and *Kailash* (mountain) were the two sacred places in Tibet visited by Hindu pilgrims every year. They carried Indian articles with them which they sold on their way to shrines. They maintained a relation of veneration with the Panchen and the Dalai Lama. Many of the Gossain traders did not come back to India but remained there for the rest of their life. Purangir Gossain was one of them. He was the most influential merchant in Tibet among the Indians. The close link with the Panchen Lama and the maintenance of a very cordial relation with the people into the higher rungs of the administrative heirarchy of Tibet enabled Purangir Gossain to enjoy comparative advantages in that country.

The influence of Indian merchants on Tibetan economy also appears to be very great.

The trade between Bengal and Tibet was conducted through Bhutan but not by merchants of Bengal. This was 'engrossed wholly by the Bhutanese'. Commodities of Bengal were conveyed into Tibet also through Murang (Terai) but being extremely hazardous, the route was abandoned. The more valuable sorts of Bengal goods were transported to Tibet by way of Muktinath Pass of Nepal also[33].

(e) *Tibet-China Trade* :

Bogle observed 'a very considerable Trade is carried on between China and Tibet'[34]. The Chinese merchants visited Tibet with their indigenous articles like coarse tea, the sale of which was 'immense', flowered and brocaded satins of various kinds, Pelong (firingi) handkerchiefs, silk thread, furs, porcelain cups, glass, snuff-boxes, knives and other cutlery, talents of silver, and tobacco. These were sold in exchange of gold, pearls, corals, chanks (shells), broad cloth, and Bengal cloth[35]. Apart from Chinese traders the Sino-Tibet trade was also carried on by the merchants of Kashmir and the agents of Panchen Lama[36].

Obviously the buyers of those Chinese assortments were Indian merchants posted in Tibet who brought them to Bengal and other places of India. The merchants of Bhutan also conducted trade with China through Tibet. They bought Chinese goods such as tea, rock salt, wool, sheep skins and other Chinese commodities in exchange of their indigenous articles like rice, wrought iron, coarse woolen cloth, and some mungit.

Most of the Chinese goods the Bhutanese merchants brought to Rangpur, a northern Bengal town, for sale. Narrow frieze was the only article which they bought for their home consumption. From Nepal they imported iron and rice[37].

The trade-route from Lhasa to China was obviously full of hazards. The route mentioned by George Bogle passed through Sinning[38] in Koknar (modern Ch'ing-hai province), but he failed to mention the route from Szechuan *via* Tachienlu. Possibly the latter was still considered primarily as a strategic military road, although later it was an important route for tea trade.

REFERENCES

1. A.M. Davies, *Warren Hastings*, P. 428 (Lond. 1936).

2. Now a district town in West Bengal.

3. *Ralph Fitch : England's pioneer to India and Burma. His companies and contemporaries with his Narrative told in his own words* ed. by Hak. Soc. Lond. 1698, P. 48. *Purchas His Pilgrims*, Vol. 1 P. 114.

4. B. Laufer, '*Was Odoric of Prodenone ever in Tibet*', pp. 405-18 (I.O.L., Lond.).

5. C. Wessels, S.J. *Early Jesuit Travellers in Central Asia* 1603-1712 (The Hague), pp. 43-68 (I.O.L., London).

6 *Ibid.*, p. 121

7. *Ibid.*, p. 164.

8. Graham Sandberg, *The Exploration of Tibet*, (Calcutta and London, 1904), pp. 32-101. But Sandberg's accuracy is questionable.

9. Father Ippolito Desideri, *An Account of Tibet*. pp. 30-32

10. P.N. Chakrabarti, *Anglo-Mughal Commercial Relations*, (Cal. 1983), P. 4 Queen Elizabeth's letter to Akbar could not be traced out.

11. Ryley, op cit., P. 98. For actual date of arrival, *Anglo-Mughal Commercial Relations* is to be consulted.

12. Ryley, P. 100.

13. W. Foster (ed.) *The English Factories in India*, 1642-45, p. 138.

14. For details see L. Petech, *The Mission of Bogle and Turner according to Tibetan Texts* (I.O.L., London).

15. C.R. Markham, ed. *Narratives of the Mission of George Bogle to Tibet and of Journey of Thomas Manning to Lhasa*, p. 124 (I.O.L., London), 1876.

16. *Ibid.*

17. Discussion can be found in W.H. Moreland, *From Akbar to Aurangzeb*, Ch. III.

18. C.R. Markham, op. cit., p. 117.

19. Sir Francis Young Husband, *India and Tibet*, p. 23, (Delhi, 1917).

20. Col. Kirkpatrick, *An Account of the Kingdom of Nepal*, p. 204 (Lond. 1811).

21. *Ibid.*, p. 372.

22. Levon Kachikian, *The Ledger of the Merchant Hevannes Joughayetsi*, Journal of the Asiatic Society, 1966, Vol. VIII, No. 3, P. 167.

23. B.H., Hodson, *Essays on the Langnages, Literatures and Religion of Nepal and Tibet together with further Papers* etc (I.O.L., London), Pt. II. Sec. VIII, (Lond. 1874), P. 97.

24. Ency : Brit., Vol. II (15th ed), Lond. 1935, p. 757.

25. C.R, Markham, op. cit. P. 129.

26. *Ibid.*

27. *Ibid.*, p. 124.

28. *Ibid.*

29. *Ibid*, pp. 44-45.

30. Gossain Merchants though Indian lived and traded in Nepal, but were expelled subsequently from there after the conquest of Nepal by the Gorkhas. Purangir Gossain, a very important Gossain merchant, took a leading part in establishing Anglo Tibet politio- Econo-

mic relations during this period. In the later part of his life he made a pilgrimage to lake Manasarovar in Westen Tibet and visited China., *Ibid* pp. 124.25.

31. *Ibid.*, pp. 56-57.

32. *Ibid.*, pp. 124-125.

33. *Ibid.*, p. 125.

34. *Ibid.*, p. 128.

35. *Ibid.*, p. 125.

36. *Ibid.*, p. 61.

37. *Ibid.*, p. 186.

38. *Ibid.*, Bogle spells it 'Seling'

CHAPTER II

I

BRITISH-CHINA COMMERCIAL RELATIONS

Several Chinese assortments like tea, gunpowder, porcelain, Chinese silk had tremendous demand in Europe. These were first brought to Genoa and were re-distributed to Northern Italy, across the Alps to South Germany and travelling through an immense network of trade routes re-distributed these assortments to Antwerp, Amsterdam, London, and Hamburg.[1] Collecting spices from Indonesian archipelago especially from Bantam, the European traders sold substantial portion of the supplies in the markets of China.[2] China was entirely dependent on Japanese copper for her minting especially during the early Manchu period, more especially during the first quarter of the eighteenth century. The Dutch East India Company, which had enjoyed exclusive rights to the European trade with Japan since 1623, made a lot of money by negotiating the export of copper from Japan to China.[3] The collapse of Antwerp market in the 1550s and the decline of this entrepot marked a turning point in London's export trade in traditional cloth.[4] Vast internal market of China and its highly profitable trade, quite naturally, tempted the European traders to grab a share of this. British commercial activities in China is essentially linked with her attempt to open the door of Tibet. The situation Britain faced in China compelled her to find an alternative land route to China in the exclusive possession of the Company resulting advantages both as a way round the restrictions of Canton and as a source of specie for remittance home from India. As the Court of Directors wrote to Bengal Government in February, 1768: 'We desire you will obtain the best intelligence you can whether trade can be opened with Nepaul, and whether cloth and other European commodities may find their way, thence to Tibet, Lhassa and the western parts of China'.[5] Now the situation faced by the English East India Company in China is to be elaborated here.

Making a basehold at Macao, in the mouth of the river Canton, the Portuguese enjoyed monopoly in China trade since 1557.[6] Hence the rivalry flared up among the European merchant adventurers, and attempts were made in every conceivable manner to find new markets. The drive to sell English textiles abroad inspired a good many trading ventures during the period of Elizabeth to north-east and north-west passages to China[7]. They made their first debut in an expedition to China in 1635 and gradually outshone other western rivals.[8]

But the task was not so easy. They faced several unsurpassable hindrances. The bulk of British foreign trade depended on the export of English cloth and wool. But the commodities found no suitable market for them in China. Therefore, either Asian products especially Indian articles to be collected to sell those to China, or gold was to be brought from England to carry on trading activities there. The system later appeared unsatisfactory. The Chinese set up a monopoly organisation to carry on trade with the Europeans.

In 1702, an individual entitled 'emperors' merchant' was appointed as the sole agent to deal with the European merchants and their trade. The system was abolished in 1771 only to be revived in 1782. Proved unsatisrfactory as it was, the system was replaced by the Co-hong, the guild of Chinese merchants engaged in foreign trade. Trully speaking, the English merchants had to carry on their trade with China in an unfavourable situation whereas the Co-hong merchants, the buffer between the European community and the Chinese official world, accrued all the benefits out of this trade. The control of both export and import lay in their hands.[9]

The language was another obstacle, over and above, the purchase of Chinese products directly from the Chinese merchants was not possible for the English merchants. From the stand point of their needs they had to appoint Chinese employees to look after their trade, whose function was like of a comprador.[10]

Again, the English merchants had to live at Canton outside the city walls during the trading season and at the end of the season the traders returned to Macao. At the beginning of the trading season they proceeded from Macao to Canton leaving their family behind.[11]

Officially English East India Company was allowed to carry on trade in China, but the English applied some mechanism what they practised in India and that was the same old abominable private trade. The students of British Indian history are, however, very much aware of consequences of private trade in India. In China the British merchants began carrying on private trade under licence of the Company. Dealing in tea they obtained enormous profit. Hence we find from 1700 onward the Company in Bengal were trying to divert their mercantile marine to China from Calcutta.[12] By the third decade of eighteenth century the tea-trade with China carried on by British merchants intensified to a great extent. Instances of withdrawing of ships from the Calcutta auction since 1723 are very frequent.[13]

Obviously the Manchu emperors disliked the private trading activities and underhand dealings of the British merchants. Naturally, the Chinese administration wanted to keep them segregated and controlled under strict regulations. But the British, in general and merchants in particular, were not at all happy for these regulations. On the contrary, they sought *laissez faire* at

least in matter of trade. Whereas the Chinese administration
were unwilling to loosen the regulations. The British historians
unfolded following reasons behind the unwillingness on the
part of the Chinese to keep or maintain friendly relations with
the Europeans.

In the first place, the Manchu emperors treated the English
as uncivilised and therefore despicable, Secondly, the Chinese
authorities were sceptical about the English who could incite
the people against Manchu rule, therefore, the English were
undesirable to the Chinese.

But a close survey of the above arguments reveal its weakness and unreasonableness.

George Bogle's report to Hastings (1775) has drawn our
attention which helps to explode the above British theories.
In that report a letter written by Tashi Lama to Bogle has been
referred to. Part of the letter necessary to our object is mentioned below:

.........'that he (Tashi Lama) had heard two Firingies being
arrived in the Deb Rajah's dominion (Bhutan),......that the
Firingies were fond of war, and after insinuating themselves
into country, raised disturbances, and made themselves masters
of it......'[14]

The above letter raises some pertinent questions :

If Tashi Lama, an inhabitant of a 'forbidden country' entirely segregated from the outer world since long came to learn
the real characteristics of the English people of the time it
was not altogether difficult for the Manchus to know about
this.

Tashi Lama could collect this information in two probable
ways; one was obviously Chinese source. He obtained the
information from the Manchus itself. It is not improbable
that the Manchus kept information about the fate of India,
that the country had been swallowed by the British merchants
who originally came there to carry on trading activities. The
suppliers of the information were undoubtedly Indian merchants who then traded with China.

The identity of second source has, however, been given by Bogle himself in his narratives. According to him, the agent of Chait Singh, the king of Benaras was sent to Tashi Lama to forewarn him about the activities of the British merchants in India. He vividly described Indian situation to Tashi Lama.

Bogle wrote in this connection :

'I had been told' by the agent of Chait Singh who described the English 'as a people designning and ambitious ; who insinuating themselves into a country on pretence of trade became acquainted with its situation and inhabitants and afterwards endeavoured to become masters of it.........'[15]

Such an accurate observation about the British activities in this part of Asia at that remote age is, however, very rare. On the other hand, the possibility of obtaining above information by the Manchus from Tashi Lama cannot be overruled. Another letter may be referred to in this connection. This letter had been written by Tashi to Taranath Lama[16] in Peking and Taranath brought this information to Manchu's notice. The requisite portion of the letter is referred to here:

'......that the English are new masters of Bengal.'[17] Whatever may be the sources of information on the part of the Chinese they rightly tackled British merchants. So the reasons mentioned above forwarded by the British historians to explain the aversion of the Manchus to the English is not true. On the otherhand the above theory tended unnecessarily spreading animosity and vilification about the Manchus.

Hardpressed by the situation the British traders had to find out an alternative trade route to China. The land route through Tibet drew their attention. The route, they thought could be brought into the exclusive possession of the Company yielding advantages both as a way round the restrictions of Canton and species for China trade could be collected from India itself.

II

PRELUDE TO BRITISH COMMERCIAL MISSION TO TIBET

The periodic British-China talks that had been going during the middle of the eighteenth century for British access to China's internal trade when proved abortive, the English East India Company had by this time obtained the *Dewani* (1765) in Bengal *Subah* comprising of Bengal, Bihar and Orissa.

In 1772, the Bhutanese, then vassals of the Tibetans, overran Kuch Behar, carried off the Raja as a prisoner, seized his country and posed a threat to the British province of Bengal which was separated from Kuch Behar by small stream only. On being insisted by the ruling authorities of Kuch Behar, the British authorities in Bengal had despatched four companies of British troops to Kuch Behar in order to thwart the Bhutanese assault. Soon the Bhutanese were driven off and Kuch Behar was annexed to Bengal. Thus, the area in North Bengal under British was extended upto the Doors in north-east India.

This fact would seem to necessitate urgent consideration to undertake new policy by the East India Company which subsequently brought about a complete change in the region's geopolitical situation. The Directors of the Company in London thought to explore the possibility of trade with the tiny

Himalayan States. The servants of the Company in Calcutta were directed from London on 16 March, 1768 to obtain all relevant information on the question whether trade could be opened with these Himalayan States.[18]

The second development involves when the Directors of the Company in London directed (1768) its Governor of Bengal to investigate the possibility of entering into China through Tibet.[16] It was this policywhich led the Company to think of sending one James Logan, a surgeon in the Company's service, towards the end of 1769, to Nepal 'to endeavour to establish a trade with Tibet and the Western Provinces of China by way of Neypall.'[20] It needs to be reaffirmed that entrance into China through Tibet could also have served the British some other additional advantages.

In the first place, the mercantilist theory propagated by Adam Smith, the ace British economist, hammered out the future possibility of exporting gold from England for China trade. Indian articles which had remarkable demand in Cnina, the British merchants thought, would have substituted the need for gold.

Secondly, the good relation between the English and Tashi Lama might offer considerable help to the former for their entrance into China's internal and foreign trade in overland route through Tibet. This consideration as a starting point for approaching the question of relations with China should help eliminate enmity and animosity.

Thirdly, it is hardly necessary to recall British desire for the cultivation of tea plants in India. This would close the necessity of importing tea from China. Western China, contiguous to Tibet, was famous for cultivation of tea plant wherefrom the seeds could easily be brought to India through Tibet.[21]

Therefore, it is found, before Warren Hasting's appointment as the Governor General of Bengal in April, 1772, the Company began thinking to establish diplomatic or commercial relations with Tibet. Hasting's desire of opening the door of

Tibet was intensified by some contemporaneous events that took place in this region and it would not be irrelevant if we throw some light on this issue.

The Gorkha invasion and conquest of Nepal sealed the prospect of India's trade with Nepal and closed the traditional India-Tibet trade route through Nepal. Asked by the Mewer king of Nepal, Jayprakash Malla, who was overthrown by the Gorkhas, for military assistance the East India Company sent an army to help Jayprakash in 1767 under Captain Kinloch.[22] Most probably it was for the first time when the English had a close view of the Himalayas. But the inhospitable region and ignorant in mountainous warfare proved to be fatal for British army. Over and above, the exigeney arose in the Deccan war against Haider Ali compelled the Company to withdraw Kinloch and his troops from Nepal and they were sent against Haider.[23]

The complete stoppage of this trade through Nepal compelled the Court of Directors to suggest the Company officials in Bengal for the exploration of Assam and Bhutan which might open a fresh channel for entrance into Tibet. Therefore, in 1773 the English Collectors posted at Rangpur and Cooch Bihar in Northern Bengal was asked to survey the prospect of Bhutan as a market for English goods.[24] The Anglo-Bhutan treaty concluded in 1772 created congenial atmosphere for this venture. But the treaty proved *fauxpas* and the renewed hostility between Bhutan and the English East India Company shattered all hopes.

Meanwhile disgusted by the interefrence of the Dev Raja Zhidar of Bhutan in the internal affairs of Cooch Bihar, the royal family fled from the kingdom. Requested by Khagendra Narayan, the Nazir Dev, to help the King to retrieve his throne the English East India Company despatched four Companies of soldiers in 1772 for the defence of Cooch Bihar under Captain Jones. Defeated at the hands of the British troops, the Bhutan King fled to his country. The defeat of Bhutan at the hands of the English East India Company and the spread of British political influence in the Himalayan region must have alarmed the Gorkha King of Nepal. He therefore, sent an envoy with a letter to Tashi Lama describing his apprehension and need to check the British before it is too late.[25]

The success of British troops against Bhutan also alarmed Tashi Lama. He, therefore sent Paima, a Tibetan and Purangir Gossain an Indian merchant *cum* pilgrim, with a letter of mediation to Warren Hastings requesting him to conclude an agreement with Bhutan on de-escalation measures to be taken along the border of Bengal and Bhutan, setting out fixed time-schedules for troop withdrawals in different sectors. The letter was received in Calcutta on March 29, 1774.[26] Accordingly treaty was signed on 25 April, 1774 between the East India Company and the Dev Raja of Bhutan.[27]

Warren Hastings, an arch imperialist, was installed, during this time as the Governor of Bengal. He was definitely well-informed about the British activities in China. At this stage, the letter of Tashi Lama which reached Calcutta in March 1774 showed Hastings the way to implement the policy he wanted to pursue in the Himalayan region.

The letter of Tashi Lama to Hastings is important document for writing the politico-economic history of the Himalayan states and the relation between India and Tibet on the one hand, and India and China, on the other. Besides number of purports may also be obtained from the letter:

Firstly, the prospect of British entrance into Tibet through Bhutan became bright.

Secondly, seeing the English giving much importance to his letter, Tashi Lama was happy and mutual understanding between them became conducive to better relations.

Thirdly, Tashi Lama's intervention brought peace in Bhutan so his influence in both Nepal and Bhutan increased to a great extent.

Subsequent events, however, proved the above purports, except the last one, useless. Tashi Lama wrote another letter to Bogle simultaneously in which he bade Bogle not to move further towards Tibet, because the Tibetans disliked it.[28] Nevertheless, Hastings thought it otherwise. Now or never was his policy and accordingly he sent a British mission comprising of George Bogle as a leader of the mission, and Alexander Hamilton, a physician. The team was approved by the Directors of the Company in London from whom Hastings sought permission to send a British Commercial Mission which should not include any Indian. Bogle stated in his narrative:

'......that they (the English servants of the Company in India) have repeatedly recommended the establishment of an intercourse with that (Tibet) country......and conceiving it to be most proper that a European, and servant of the Company should be entrusted with the negotiation in preference to any native......'[29]

Purangir was detained to show the English mission way to Tibet and he was waiting in Calcutta for that.

Eventually an appointment letter was issued to Goerge Bogle on May 13, 1774 making him the leader of the first British Commercial Mission to Tibet. The object of the mission has been elaborately delineated in that letter. It runs :

'Sir,

Having appointed you my (Hastings') deputy to the Tashi Lama, the sovereign of Bhutan[30], I desire you proceed to Lhasa......

The design of your mission is to open a mutual and equal communication of trade between the inhabitants of Bhutan and Bengal...you will take with you samples of a trial of such articles of commerce as may be sent......'

'You will inquire what other commodities may be successfully employed in that trade. And you will diligently inform yourself of the manufacturers, productions, goods introduced by the intercourse with other countries, which are to be procured in Bhutan, especially as are of great value and easy transportation, such as gold, silver, precious stones, musk, rhubark

(Rawend), munjit (a madder used as a dye, and also for medical purposes).

'The following will be also proper objects of your inquiry-the nature of the road between the borders of Bengal and Lhasa, and of the countries lying between; the communications between Lhasa and the neighbouring countries, their government revenue and manners.'[31]

Apart from these instructions mentioned in his appointment letter he was also instructed privately to enquire what countries lie between Lhasa and Siberia and what communication there is between them. The same with regard to China and Kashmir.[32] It is interesting to note that Hastings showed his interest on Siberia.

In addition to these Bogle was given a memorandum containing geographical and historical informations about Tibet.

Though apparently the informations are not always correct nevertheless it examined the Sino-Tibet political relations since thirteenth century. A close examination of the memorandum will reveal some British ideas and conceptions about the Chinese in particular. The Memorandum narrates : 'Although the Chinese historians ascribe to their emperors the power of nominating the Dalai Lama, it does not follow that this nomination is more than a bare acknowledgement or confirmation of his appointment by the Lamas or Tibetan tribes. It may likewise not be improbable that the Typa Lama is chosen by the priest. It is atleast, generally said that the chiefs of the Tibetan tribes that acknowledge a sort of supremacy in the Dalai Lama are all elected by the priests, or Lamas, nobility at the same time having some influence in the transaction.'[33] Subsequent event will prove this observation is correct. Notwithstanding this fact, it would be seen that the British in India never opposed the Chinese illegal activities in Tibet, and their propagation that Tibet was her protectorate.

Again, Bogle was advised to collect information about 'any fact relative to the State of Tibet with respect to China and Tatary...or whereas the Dalai Lama is still a vassal to China'.[34]

Thus it appears that in spite of writing by TashiLama himself to Hastings describing Tibet was a vassal to China, Hastings had a doubt about its authenticity. Bogle, however, set out in the middle of may, 1774. The British attempt to collect information on Tibet through Bogle and his meticulous collection of information is extremely valuable to determine the relation between Tibet and China. Discussion on it has been done later on.

Even after collecting all the required informations about China's relation with Tibet, which was essentially full of hatred, trading charges, holding one another responsible for the carnage often done by both sides posing threats of serious breach of peace in the Himalayan region, the British authorities in India remained silent. The reasons are not far to seek and the discussion of which would be made later on. It is now important here to discuss in detail about other British commercial missions followed Bogle afterwards.

REFERENCES

1. C.M. Cipolla, '*The Fontana Economic History of Europe*, Vol. 2, p. 494.

2. *Ibid.*, p. 448

3. *Ibid.*, p. 498

4. *Ibid.*, p. 508

5. *Home Miscellaneous* (I.O.L., London), Vol. 219, P. 325

6. Harold M. Vinacke, *A History of the Far East in Modern Times* (Lond. 1960), p. 29.

7. *Ibid.*, p. 33

8. *Ibid.*,

9. *Ibid.*, p. 32

10. *Ibid.*

11. *Ibid.*

12. Holden Furber, *The Growth of British Power in India* published in India Past and Present, Vol. No. 1, 1984, p. 51. It is well known that private trade of the East India Company's servants, involving use of the rermits, grew to be a grave anamoly in India's economic history in the eighteenth century. Balkrishna, *Commercial Relations*

between India and England', pp. 77-79 ; Prof. J.N. Sarkar, '*Life of Mirjumla*'. Private and privileged trade between China and servants of the English East India Company developed to great extent by 1740. It was actually a disguised expansion of private trade on the Company shipping. It stimulated British commanded country-voyages from Indian ports to the China sea*s. India office Records, Correspondence Reports,* 3, July 9, 1720.

13. *Ibid.* It should be remembered, the Company alone was not bene-ficiary of its Tibet Policy. Pitt's India Act of 1784 set up a joint con:rol Policy by the British government.

14. Bogle, *op cit.,* p.131

15. *Ibid.*

16. Chidzun Lama then was at Peking, identical with the Taranath Lama (is the third Pontiff of the Yellow Cap, Geluckpa sect) ; the Dalai and Tashi being the other two. Taranath resided north of Tibet, among the Khalka tribes of outer Mongolia near Urga. Several visits of Taranath Lama to Peking are recorded. *Hakluyat Society,* Vol. 1, p. 98. It may be that Bogle coufuses Chidzum Lama or Gulson Tamba with the Changay Lama.

17. Bogle, *op. cit.,* p. 131.

18. *Home Dept. Consultations,* 9 Dec. 1771.

19. *Home Miscellaneous* (I.O.L., London), Vol. 219, p. 325.

20. S.C. Sarkar, *Some notes on the Intercourse of Bengal,* an article published in the Proc. of the IHRC, Vol. XIII, 1930, p. 184.

21. *Bengal Public Consultation,* No. 17, Jan, 13, 1790 (Indian Arcnives, New Delhi).

22. K.C. Chaudhuri, *Anglo-Nepalese Relations* (Cal. 1950), pp. 13-33.

23. *Ibid.,* p. 33.

24. *Proc. IHRC,* Vol. XIII (1930), P. 104.

25. Bogle Papers (IOL, London) EUR. MSS. E/226 *Hamilton to Hastings,* 30 May, 1776.

26. C.U. Aitchison, *Treaties, Engagements and Sanads,* Vol. II, p. 189.

27. *Ibid.* In the treaty Tibet should have been included because Bhutan was her vassal, and this leads us to think th t Tibet lacked political knowledge. Tashi Lama was wrongly stated as the sovereign of Bhutan.

28. Bogle, *op., cit,* p.131.

29. *Ibid.* p. 4,

30. *Home Misc Vol. 219,* p. 425

31. Teshu Lama or Tashi Lama better known as Panchen Lama was neither soverign of Bhutan, nor of Tibet.

32. Bogle, *op cit.* p. 6

33. *Ibid.,* p. 8

34. *Ibid.,* p. 10

35. *Ibid.,* p. 12.

Part II

Direct Commercial Contact

Part II

Direct Commercial Contact

CHAPTER III

I

OFFICIAL ATTEMPTS

(A) *British Commercial Missions to Tibet*

Entry of the English East India Company into free trade of China by sea being impossible, the Company resolved to explore the route to China through Tibet. A land route to China in the exclusive possession of the Company had obvious advantages. Firstly, Tibet bought more Indian goods than it sold, and the payment was made in gold and silver.

Secondly, this would replenish the demand for specie in the China trade.

Thirdly, the route will serve as a way round the restrictions of Canton.

The period from 1774 to 1811 witnessed altogether nine official and one unofficial commercial missions sent by the English East India Company to Nepal Bhutan and Tibet. Two-fold methods were taken up.

In the first place, the Company desired to establish a close relation with the Tashi Lama of Tibet.

Secondly, as the influence of the Lama at the court of China was also much strengthened, so the Company thought to influence Chinese Court by the Lama. Warren Hastings, the first Governor General of Bengal stated in this connection, 'By means of Teshoo Lama therefore I am inclined to hope that a communication may be opened with the Court of Peking either through his mediation or by an agent directly from this government'[2] (East India Company's Government).

Among the missions there were again Europeans and Indians. The number of Missions will reveal itself the exigency that the English Company felt for Intra-Asian Country trade through the Himalayas.

The first mission was sent to Tibet in 1774 headed by George Bogle 'a servant of the Company well known for his assiduity, intelligence and exactions in affairs, as well as for the coolness and moderation of temper which he seemed to 'possess in an eminent degree'[3]. His mission, as is suggested by Hastings was to open a 'mutual and equal communication of trade between Tibet and Bengal'.

If we closely review the appointment letter given to Bogle on 13th May, 1774, by Hastings from Fort William it will be found that the letter contains some erroneous remarks.

Bhutan is referred to as the place where Bogle would go. But actually the place would be Bhot, the native name of Tibet and not Bhutan.

Secondly, Tashi Lama who has been described as Teshu Lamboo and the ruler of Bhutan was actually one of the occupants of the four chairs of the Chemiling, Tenjiling, Chechuling and Kenduling monasteries of Tibet. He resided at Tashilhumpo and was better known as Panchen Lama[4].

The second mission that followed Bogle headed by Mr. Alexander Hamilton, a physician, who was also a member of Bogle's mission set out for Tibet towards the end of 1773 to investigate conditions of trade through the country and to try to keep in touch with Tibet. But the Tibetan hierarchy in Lhasa did not allow him to enter into Tibet so he had to come back from Bhutan.[5]

The third mission led again by Hamilton in 1777 bore no fruit. Hamilton's letter to Hastings in May 1778 expresses his feelings for his failure to enter into Tibet. He wrote, 'from the particular situation of affairs at Tashilhumpo and the unreasonable jealousy of the Lhasa government the expectation I had formed of visiting Thibet are now at an end.[6]

The fourth mission headed by the same George Bogle, was prepared to go to Tibet. The internal situation of Tibet also encouraged the Company. The Regent who was thought to have been hostile to the English now died. Bogle was instructed to 'endeavour by the means of the Lamas of Thibet to open a communication with the Court of Peking and if possible procure leave to poceed ţthither'[7]. But Bogle's Journey was postponed due to the news received in Calcutta that the Tashi Lama was about to set out for China. Later the Company authorities in Calcutta received the information that the Lama had died of small pox in Peking in 1780.[8] Bogle also died after a few months in Calcutta.[9]

Again the curtain was raised in 1782. This time the task was entrusted to Captain Samuel Turner, a military officer of the Company in Bengal and a kinsman of Hastings. He led the fifth mission. S. Davis of the Bengal Engineers and R. Saunders, the physician were other two Englishmen who accompanied Turner.[10]

Purangir Gossain headed the sixth mission in 1785. By the time Purangir returned to India, Hastings had already set out for England[11].

Col. Kirkpatrick headed the seventh mission in 1793. But this mission went to Nepal instead of to Tibet.[12] Kirkpatrick was followed by Maulana Abdul Qadir who headed the eighth mission to Nepal in 1795-96. Ha was sent to open the route to China through Nepal. But his attempts were foiled by the Tibetans. The failure of all Missions led by English men except Bogle and Turner perhaps prompted the British in India to send mission intermittently led by Indians. Moreover, the tract, land language and customs were unfamiliar to the British. Abdul Qadir suggested that European goods for trade with Tibet

should be brought just near the border of Tibet if Indian traders were not allowed to enter into Tibet.[13]

Remaining silent for a couple of years the Company again
sent Captain Knox as the first British Resident at Katmandu
in 1810. He was specially instructed to 'cause complete effect to
be given to the operation of the Treaty of Commerce concluded
between the Company and the Nepal Government in 1790.'[14]

The last and only unofficial mission was headed by Mr.
Manning in 1811, who was not recognised agent of British
Government in India, but a private adventurer who went up
in spite of and against the wishes of the Government.

After Manning no Englishman in either a private or official
capacity, visited Lhasa till the mission of 1904.

It is evident that the Company remained silent from 1811
to 1904 in connection with Tibet. We will try to throw some
light on the reason of this aloofness. But prior to that the
activities and impacts of each and every mission need to be
anatomised in order to have a clear idea about India-Tibet-
China's politico-economic relations.

Returning from Tibet Bogle submitted his report along with
an 'account of travelling charges incurred on his expedition to
Thibet.' From which he deducted the amount equivalent to the
presentation made to him by the Lama and other dignitaries
of Tibet. The Company authorities in Bengal were so happy by
the execution of responsibility entrusted to Bogle that an order
was given 'to allow him a salary of 1200 rupees per month for
the period of his absence.' The Company also showed the
generosity of granting him 9063 rupees as a reimbursement
of his expenditure.[16]

On 16th April, 1777, the Board of Directors of the East
India Company informed the Company authorities in Bengal
that they 'are glad to find that effectual methods have been
adopted to open a communication with the Government of
Thibet by the agency of Mr. Bogle who appears to have been
a person well qualified for the employment, and to trade

acquited himself to your satisfaction.' The Board of Directors were glad to see that Bogle had punctually submitted his account along with the statement of presents he received 'in his embassy'. The Board fully 'approved of the salary of Rupees 1200 per month allowed him during his absence... .' Finally the Board expressed its hope that the Company officials in Bengal would 'take every occasion to continue a correspondence so happily begun with the Lama.'[17]

Tashi Lama requested Bogle to arrange a piece of land in Calcutta on the bank of the Ganges to erect a Buddhist temple. The request was approved and the Company in Bengal was directed 'to make the grant in such a manner as may be most expressive of our (Company's) good disposition towards him.'[18]

But Bogle's journey to Tibet was a difficult one. Even before he had reached the capital of Bhutan, he received a letter from Tashi Lama in which the Lama apprised Bogle that as Tibet was subject to the Emperor of China, who had ordered that no Mughal, Indian, Pathan or Englishman should be admitted to Tibet. The Lama wrote further that distance between Tibet and China was so long that permission of Chinese Emperor could not be brought easily and early. Therefore, Bogle should return to Calcutta.[19]

The letter is very interesting from several points of view. For the first time official declaration had been made that Tibet was a subject state of China.

Secondly, it cleared Tashi Lama's position.

Thirdly, the king of Bhutan refused to intercede on his behalf, Bogle put all reliance on Purangir to obtain permission for him.

Now we will check and recheck to see how far Tashi Lama's letter contain correct information. The letter, however, signifies that the Tibetans were obviously reluctant to allow the Europeans into their country. The reference to the Chinese sovereignty is mentioned here only to exaggerate the degree of Manchu control in order to impress Bogle. Evidently, the Lama wanted to expose his innocence and tried to shift entire responsibility on the shoulder of the Chinese. This was deliberately done because of fear of the English arms and their design to extend British sovereignty towards the Himalayan region.

The Chinese were undoubtedly unaware of it. And it is surprising that the English East India Company did not try to clarify the actual position of Tibet but believed the theory advanced by the Lama. Hastings, in a consultation maintained that the 'country of Tibbet is subject to the Emperor of China, Two Chinese Viceroys, appointed by the Court of Peking resided at Lhasa......'.[20] This is the root of many complications in the subsequent years.

Meanwhile the repeated encroachment of the British Commercial Missions on its way to Tibet through Bhutan irritated the Dev Raja Jigme Sengye. In December 1778 he sent one Nirpur Paiga to Hastings with a letter, in which he alleged that this won't be tolerated. In clear and unmistakable terms, he informed Hastings that he must not allow any English or European to travel through his country. In addition to this the Bhutani envoy put up some boundary disputes which they thought unfavourable to Bhutan. Hastily the dispute was settled giving some privileges to Bhutan apparently to make content its king.[21]

The above incident makes it clear that the British administration in Bengal committed a blunder by not inserting the term of free passage to Tibet through Bhutan in the agreement of 1779.

From the Minute submitted by the Governor General of Bengal before the Board of Directors in London some new informations are gleaned, by which new light can be thrown on reasons of arranging to send further British missions to Tibet despite the restriction imposed on them from entering Bhutan and Tibet.

The Minute runs that the constant drain of money from these provinces (Bengal *subah*) 'is a consequence naturally arising from the relative situation in which this country is placed with respect to Great Britain and as the sources from which money flows into Bengal are known to be very disproportionate, this evil has been repeatedly pointed out as of the most alarming kind.'[22]

In all probability, this drain was due to financing the China trade of the Company. Now the actual motive of the English for trying to open up the door of Tibet exposed, when Hastings wrote in his Minute:

'......Teshu Lama's Interest (relation) at the Court of China is also much strengthened by a strict friendship which subsists between him and Changea Lama the priest immediatly attendant on the person of the Emperor, who from his great age and character is held in much respect at Pekin.

'By means of Teshu Lama therefore I am inclined to hope that a communication may be opened with the court of Pekin either through his mediation or by an agent directly from this government' (Bengal Government).[23]

Hastings, therefore, thought it imperative to send immediately British commercial missions to Tibet. But his previous experience in this respect was not at all satisfactory. The second and third missions were not allowed to enter into Tibet. So he thought of sending Bogle again. In this connection he mentioned in his Minute:

'On these grounds I beg leave to recommend that Mr. Bogle be appointed to proceed again into Bootan and Tibet with instructions to cultivate and improve the good understanding subsisting between the chiefs of those countries and this government to endeavour to establish a free and lasting intercourse of Trade with the kingdom of Tibet .....'[24]

And this was not the ultimate end of Hastings' efforts. Because the same Minute states that 'by the means of the Lamas of Tibet to open a communication with the Court of Pekin and if possible procure to leave to proceed thither.......'

                                Signed/Warren Hastings
1 agree   Signed/Richard Barwell
1 agree   Signed/Eyre Coote[25]

It has, however, already mentioned that Bogle's journey was adjourned. Though Bogle could not proceed towards Tibet, he could have performed a formidable task **on** behalf of the Company if he did not die a premature death.

Before he set out for Tibet Purangir was contacted who was then in Tashilhumpo to communicate with Tashi Lama. From there he informed the Company that the Lama requested Bogle to proceed to Canton by sea where he would meet Bogle and the Lama would take him to Peking.[26] But all the attempts of the English were frustrated due to Lama's death in Peking.

Turn of Turner came and he was no inferior to Bogle. The installation of the new Lama provided Hastings an opportunity to send Turner just as an English representative on this auspicious occasion. He spent nearly a year in Tibet. But nothing tangible could be produced. He remained at Shigatse and could not proceed further due to anti-English attitude of the Tibetans. He had to return from Shigatse[72]. Returning from Shigatse, Turner suggested the Company to send a group of Indian merchants to Tibet which could repair the rift betwen the Tibetans and the English East India Company. Accordingly Hastings instructed in April 1784 to circulate an advertisement inviting Indian merchants to carry on trade with Tibet. The party of merchants was asked to assemble in February 1785 with the following articles :

Second quality cloth, coating, cheap watches, clocks, trinkets, snuff-Boxes, smelling bottles, pocket knives, amber, gloves and coarse cottons. The articles were to be exempted from all duties.[28] Hastings wrote to the members of the Council to approve this plan. His letter runs :

Lucknow 22 April 1784

'Edward Wheeler Esqre & Council Fort William,
Gentlemen

I beg leave to recommend to your consideration a plan delivered to me by Mr. Turner for the trial of trade between Bengal and Tibet. If it meets with your approbation I would further propose that it be published by advertisement with an Invitation to the native merchants of Bengal to engage in it, and an exemption of the Duties of such Articles as shall compose their first adventure.

Signed   Warren Hastings
Advertisement was published but the medium is not known.
'Advertizement

......a promise of encouragement to all Merchants Natives of India, who may be sent to Traffic in Thibet on behalf of the government of Bengal and a promise of yielding them every Assistance requisite for the transport of their „goods from the frontier of Bhootan, and of assigning them a place of Residence either within the Monastery, or should it be considered as more eligible in the town, the Native merchants of Bengal are hereby informed thereof, and invited to engage in the trade receiving as they hereby do, the promise of this Government, that their shall be an exemption of all Duties upon such articles as shall be taken out of Bengal to compose their first Adventure to Thibet......

It is proposed that the Natives employed on this service should assemble with their goods or Rungpore early in the month of February......

Fort William
Political Department
11th May 1774

Published by
order of the Honb'le the
Governor General and Council
(Signed) E. Hay, Secretary'[29]

It is not, however, known whether the Indian merchants were at all sent or not or what was the impact of such mission. But the idea was novel no doubt.

However, Hastings had left India by this time and Macpherson was a temporary Governor General in place of Hastings. He believed that trade with China through Tibet was possible and the repeated attempts would be successful.[30]

We know the Sixth mission headed by Col. Kirkpatrick but the mission went to Nepal instead of Tibet. To know the reason we will have to trace back.

The conclusion of Anglo-Bhutanese war by the treaty signed and ratified on April 1774 enabled Company to annex Cooch-

Behar to the province of Bengal. The annexation as it is stated earlier, had offered the Company to extend its political influence towards the Eastern Himalayan region.

The Bhutanese must have considered the English aggression on their land as an unwarranted interference in their internal affairs. The English army sent against the Gorkha Raja in 1767 accomplished nothing except arousing the hostility of the Gorkhas. This also created an alarm among the Bhutanese for which they did not want to assist Bogle in his journey to Tibet. The conquest of India, the annexation of Cooch-Behar, the war against the Gorkha Raja and the expedition against Bhutan made the people of the Himalayas understand that trade in the hands of the English became a vehicle of imperialistic activities.

Bogle realised the futility of English aggression against Bhutan and Nepal and criticised the war-efforts of the British against Bhutan in particular, in strongest term.[31] His remarks in this connection are worth-quoting directly.

'Attempting (to take possession of Bhutan) by force will never answer. The difficulties are unsurmountable atleast without a force and expense much greater than the object is worth. This does not arise from the power of the Bhutanese. Two battalions, I think could reduce their country, but two brigades could not keep communication open, and that if that is cut off the conquest could be of no use'.

Then Bogle turned his attention towards company's war against Nepal and observed :

'In all the schemes that I have heard of for an expedition to Nepal, this has been overlooked, on a supposition that if conquest was effected all the rest would follow of course ; but that I am convinced would not be the case when the natural strength of the country is considered, this would appear still more forcibly. For these reasons, I am no advocate for an expedition into these countries unless the people should commence hostilities and then it should be done only with a view to reduce them to peace on such terms as should appear honourable and advantageous to the Company ; and this would be easily effected by acting vigorously for one season.

'The objections I have made against expedition into Bhutan hold good with respect to Nepal and Lhasa, for this sole reason that a communication can not be kept open ; and should our troops march into these countries, they must consider all communication with the low country out of the question will they return.'[32]

From the above observations it comes to our notice that the aggressive attitude of the English in this part of India had some inherent weaknesses and at the same time it might not have escaped the attention of the peoples of this hilly region. It would have been difficult for the English in Bengal to convince Nepal, Bhutan or Tibet that such an aggressive policy might not some day be directed against them. Hence, Nepal and Tibet wholeheartedly tried to keep the English out of their respective countries.

Nepal, on the other hand, also decided to expand its domain towards northern Bengal with the obvious intention of showing her might lest the English should direct their invasion towards Nepal. By 1780, Prithvi Narayan, king of Nepal, occupied Morang, a tract of 271 square miles between the rivers Mechi .and Mahananda just adjacent to the Company's districts of Rangpur and Purnea. But this utterly maladroit move proved unsuccessful. Soon Nepal was engaged in war with China and this brought her all misfortunes.

REFERENCES

1. Home Miscellaneous (India Office Library, Londan) Vol. 219, p. 385
2. *Ibid.* p. 386
3. *Ibid.*, p. 387.
4. *Ibid.*, Vol. 608 f. 33
5. Bogle Papers (IOL. London),: Hamilton to Hastings 30 May 1776
6. *Ibid.*, H.M., Vol. 219, p. 373
7. H.M. Vol. 219, 387
8. S. Cammann, *The Panchen Lama's visit to China in 1780* (IOL, London); S. Cammann. *Trade through the Himalayas,* Far

Eastern Quarterly Vol. IX (IOL. London). There was a rumour that Tashi Lama had been murdered by the Chinese because of the friendship he had shown to the English E.I. Co.

9. H.M., Vol. 219, p. 379

10. *Ibid.*, Vol. 608. f 33

11. *Ibid.*

12. Col. Kirk Patrick, *An Account of the kingdom of Nepaul* (IOL. London) pp. 371-9 Lond, 1811.

13. K.C. Chaudhuri, *Anglo-Nepalese Relations* p. 75 Cal. 1960

14. B.D. Sanwal, *Nepal and theE.I. Co.* pp. 91-95, Bombay, 1965

15. Sarat Chandra Das wrote a letter to the Dalai Lama in 1878 asking permission to visit that city. He also wrote another letter to the Panchen Lama of Tashi-l-humpo with a like request. Both of them sent him a favourable reply together with a passport to travel through the southern province of Tsang to Tashilhumpo. On being requested to teach him the use of the extant, prismatic compass, etc. and how to note thefeatures of mountaneous countries the Surveyor-General deputed one Nain Singh to teach Sarat Candra Das all these lessons. Sarat Chandra was the Headmaster of the Bhutia School at Darjeeling Vide Graham Sandberg, *The Exploration of Tibet, its history and Particulars*, Lord, 1904, P. 164.

16. H.M. Vol. 219. p. 375

17. *Ibid.*, p, 377

18. *Ibid.*, p. 378

19. Bogle Papers : Tashi Lama to Hastings, 22 July, 1775

20. H.M. Vol. 219, pp. 384-85

21. Governor General Proceedings (IOL London) 6 Aprl, 1779, pp, 2-6

22. H.M., Vol. 219, p. 379

23. *Ibid*

24. *Ibid.*, p. 384

25. *Ibid*

26. *Ibid*

27. *Ibld*, Vol. 608. (IOL London), f. 33

28. *Ibid*,

29. *Ibid*, Vol. 219

30. *Ibid* Vol. 688, f. 33

31. Narrative of the Mission of George Bogle to Tibet and Journey of Thomas Manning to Lhasa (London). ed by Clement R. Markham, pp. 56-57. London 1876

32. *Ibid*, pp. 57-58

33. H.M. Vol. 608

II

UNOFFICIAL ATTEMPTS

(a) *Thomas Manning*

India's modern attempt to know Tibet started with George Bogle's attempt to explore her in 1774 and ended with Thomas Manning, an English physician, who went to Lhasa in 1811 on his own initiative.[1] Details of his journey and his activities in Tibet are found in the *'Narratives of the Mission of G. Bogal......and of the Journey of Thomas Manning to Lhasa'* edited by G.R. Markham. Sir Francis Younghusband, the leader of British expedition in Tibet in 1904, has described in his book *'India and Tibet'*, some details about Manning's activities in Tibet which, he admitted, collected from Manning's *Diary*. The *Diary* and the *Narratives* are, most probably, identical.

From the *Narratives* we come to learn that Manning went to Tibet *via* Bhutan. He was not an accredited agent of Government but a private adventurer, and he went up inspite of, and against the wishes of the Government of India of the time. He had a very sound knowledge in Chinese. He studied in England and France, then went to Canton and remained there for three years. Armed with a letter of introduction from the Select Committee of Canton to Lord Minto, the British Governor General of India, asking to give him every possible assistance in his attempt to go to Tibet, he came to India. Receiving no aid he took recourse to his own initiative and went to Lhasa. Escorted by a Chinese servant he arrived at Phari at the head of the Chumbi Valley on October 21, 1811. Description of Phari given by Manning, is classic : 'Dirt, grease, smoke, Misery, but good mutton. Giving two bottles of cherry-brandy and a wine glass, he greeted the Chinese Mandarin who arrived there from Gyantse to meet

Manning. The Mandarin invited him in the dinner and pledged to write to the Lhasa Mandarin for permission for Manning to proceed to Lhasa. Manning healed a number of Chinese soldiers by medical treatment. His medicines, 'did wonderfully well, and the patients were very greatful'. The soldiers requested the Mandarin to take Manning with him to Gyantse which he agreed.

Manning made a very favourable impression on the Chinese who he remarked ruled Tibet like the English in India and 'made the Tibetans stand before them'. He, however, considered the presence of the Chinese in Tibet was fruitful and advantageous to the English in India. 'Things are much pleasanter now the Chinese are here', he says, 'the Magistrate hints about overtures respecting opening a commercial intercourse between the Chinese and the English through Bhutan. I cannot help exclaiming in my mind (as I often do) what fools the Company are to give me no commission, no authority no instructions. What use are their Embassies when their Ambassadors cannot speak to a soul and can only make ordinary phrases pass through a stupid interpreter ? No *finesse* no *tarture*, no compliments. Fools, fools, fools, to neglect an opportunity they may never have again !'

Manning travelled to Gyantse in great discomfort because of very severe cold. The vicious horse which kicked and bit him all along the way, had a saddle highly uncomfortable so he changed pony one after another. The second one 'sprang forward in a full runaway gallop, with the most furious and awkward motion (he) ever experienced' : and the third one was 'so weak so tottering and so stumbling, and trembled so whenever he set his foot on a stone, which was about every other step', that he could 'hardly keep up with the company'. Reaching Gyantse he was, however, treated with great courtesy. He was lodged in a hut and supplied with his requirements. The Chinese soldiers who needed medical treatment from him gave him what he wanted, 'One brought rice, one brought meat, another brought a cake, another brought a little paste and pepper and mended a hole in the window, another brought a present of a pen and candles'. Chinese inhabitants of the town came to see him and the Chinese General who invited him to dinner was 'vastly civil and polite'. Though the Chinese general was 'very much of a gentleman', Manning concluded that he was really 'no better than an old woman. The dinner was tolerably good, and the wine excellent, but the cooking was indifferent.' The General's impression on Manning, on the whole, was good. He was impressed by Manning's beard and declared that he had never seen one nearly so handsome.

From Manning's description we come to learn that beside the Chinese Mandarin there was a 'Tibet Mandarin' who lived 'in a sort of castle on the top of a hill'. He also visited him and talked for half an hour, but Manning did not keep a record of the discussion. The Chinese General, however, sought permission from Lhasa authorities to permit Manning to go to Lhasa and the permission arrived a few days after his arrival at Gyantse. He was given a passport, transport and necessary supplies were furnished. As he approached near Lhasa he was met by a 'respectable person on horse back, who dismounted and saluted' him. The man was sent by the Tibetan authorities to welcome him and escort him to Lhasa.

The town of Lhasa failed to impress Manning, which had 'nothing striking, nothing pleasing, in its appearance......In short everything seemed mean and gloomy, and excited the idea of something unreal'. At Lhasa his first task was to pay his respects not to the Tibetan but to the Chinese Mandarin, and afterwards he visited the 'Chief Tibetan officials'.

On December 17, 1811, he went to the Potala to salute the Grand Lama. He took with him as an offering 'broadcloth two pair of China ewers, a pair of good brass candlesticks, thirty new bright dollars , as many pieces of zinc, some genuine Smith's lavender-water......... a good store Nankin tea, which is a rarity and delicacy at Lhasa, and not to be brought there.' The little Grand Lama was seven years old. The Lama made a few remarks to Manning in Tibetan which was interpreted in Chinese to Manning's Chinese Munshi, and the Munshi in Latin to Manning. He was so much overwhelmed by the sight of the Grand Lama that he 'could have wept through strangeness of sensation'.

Both the Chinese and the Tibtans treated him with great respect in Lhasa, nevertheless, there were some who spied upon Manning: He remarked that 'my bile used to rise when the hounds looked into my room.' However, he passed several months at Lhasa where, on the whole, he was not, badly treated. Commanded eventually by the Chinese authorities in Peking he had to leave Tibet. He left Lhasa on April 19, and reached Kuch Behar on June 10, 1812.

For about seven months Manning remained in Tibet and all these time he did nothing except healing diseases and paying many visits to the Grand Lama. His object of going to Tibet was a 'moral view of China, its manners, the degree of happiness the people enjoy, their sentiments and opinions so far as they influence life, their literature, their history, the causes of their stability and vast population, their minor arts and contrivances; what there might be in China to serve as a model for imitation, and what to serve as a beacon to a void'. But it is difficult to perceive from the writings of Manning that how it was possible for him to take 'a moral view of China' going to Tibet. So it appears that he had a mind to go to China through Tibet and for which he learnt Chinese.

Giving much importance to the memoir of Manning, Sir Francis Younghusband has described 'it is a meagre record of so important a journey'. We glean some facts of relation between Tibet and China from the memoir if we examine it critically.

Firstly, permission in every stage of his entrance from one town to the other, from Phari to Gyantse and from Gyantse to Lhasa was obtained from the Chinese Mandarin and not from the Tibetan hierarchy which evidently proves that the Chinese had firmly established political control over Tibet. The Chinese overlordship is more apparent when Manning remarks that the Chinese officials in Tibet 'made the Tibetans stand before them' and ruled Tibet like the English in India. It leads us to believe that the Chinese forcefully imposed their political hegemony on Tibet during the period of our discussion.

Secondly, his entrance to Lhasa was, however, permitted by the Tibetan 'Magistrate' of Lhasa and a Passport was given by him. It reveals that to enter into Lhasa a foreigner did not need permission from the Chinese officials stationed at Lhasa. This is really peculiar particularly when we consider the unilateral demand of the Chinese of Tibet.

Thirdly, the Chinese officials in Tibet were in favour of establishing British-China commercial relations while the Peking authorities were afraid of the British power in India for which Manning was ordered to leave Tibet.

Fourthly, Manning found a large number of Chinese inhabitants in Lhasa and its adjoining places. They were, as is understood from Manning's observation, 'bad-charactered' people. This leads us to believe that Chinese Government might have used Tibet as deporting centre for convicted Chinese crminals.

Last but not the least, the Tibeto-Chinese relation did not escape Manning's notice and he therw sufficient light on it. Manning confirmed that, while Tibetans dreaded the Chinese, they disliked them intensely. He observes that the 'Chinese are very distrustful to the Tibetans. Only bad-charactered Chinese were sent to Tibet,' and he could not help thinking that the Tibetans would, view the Chinese influence in Tibet overthrown without many emotions of regret, especially if the rulers under the new influence were to treat the Grand Lama with respect, for this is a point in which those haughty Mandarins are somewhat deficient, to the no small dissatisfaction of the good people of Lhasa.'

The Chinese impression about the English can also be found from the remarks made by the Chinese General in Tibet. On one occasion he observed 'These Europeans are very formidable; now one man (Manning) has come to spy the country he will inform others. Numbers will come, and at last they will be for taking the country from us.'[3]

Amongst all the above three English visitors of Tibet namely Bogle, Turner and Manning, the last one was familiar with the Chinese language. He studied it in France and England and then he made his way to Canton, remained there three years. It is surprising to note that despite his knowledge in Chinese he kept the matter secret during his stay in Tibet and allowed the Chinese Munshi to translate him into Latin. After Manning no other English man visited Lhasa till Younghusband expedition of 1904.

William Moorcroft, is another enterprising Englishman is said to have gone to Tibet in 1812 despite Company's restriction but whether could reach his destination is not known.[4]

But the efforts to explore Tibet was not ceased altogether. A list of explorers of different national is given below :

British		*French*	
1.	Richard	1.	Huc
2.	Henry Strachey	2.	Gabet
3.	Carey	3.	Bonavolot
4.	Littledale	4.	Prince Henri d' Orleans
5.	Bower	5.	Dutreuil de Rhins
6.	Wellby	6.	Grenard
7.	Deasy		
8.	Rawling		

Russian		*Indian*	
1.	Prjevalsky	1.	Sarat Chandra Das
2.	Pievtsoff		
3.	Kozoloff		

REFERENCE

1. At Combridge he was the friend of Charles Lamb, became Second Wrangler, but he was a man of 'eccentric nature' and left the university without a degree. He had an inordinate passion to go to China and Tibet and therefore learnt China in France and England. The Select Committee of the English East India Company in Canton gave him a letter of introduction to Lord Minto, the contemporary Governor-General of India, requesting him to provide all sorts of possible assistance to Manning for his journey to Tibet. But he was not given any help for reason not known.

2. The palace Potala by name was the official residence of the Dalai Lama.

3. The observation is surprisingly correct. It appears that the Tibetans did know the fate of India.

4. Moorcroft explord western Tibet, and according to Younghusband, he actually reached Lhasa and died there. Sir Francis Younghusband, *India and Tibet*, p. 40.

III

GORKHA INVASION OF TIBET

In July, 1788 Nepal invaded Tibet and Sikkim. Hardpressed by the Nepalese troops Tibet at once sought Military assistance from English East India Company against Nepal. Lord Cornwallis, who was then Governor General of Bengal, declined to comply with the request on the plea of long distance between Calcutta and Lhasa.[2]

The unwillingness on the part of Cornwallis to help Tibet against Nepal was criticised later on. The reasons of unwillingness as they are found in Macartney Papers are as follows :—

   (i) This would go against 'the general policy of the British Government' ;

   (ii) This would be 'inconsistant with connection that has so long prevailed between the Company and the (Chinese) Emperor' and

   (iii) The distance between Calcutta and Lhasa was 'considerable'.[3]

If we review Cornwallis' unwillingness closely some more reasons could be found.

If the first place, Cornwallis' reluctance to interfere into Sino-Nepal Warfare should be traced to the policy pursued by his predecessor Hastings who was advised by Dr. B. Hamilton, a counsellor to his Government on Himalayan matters, not to wage war against Nepal or occupy her. He pointed out, 'a British occupation of Nepal would create an extremely long Sino-British Border.........a frontier of 7 or 8 hundred miles between two powerful nations holding each other in mutual contempt seems to point at anything but peace'.[4]

George Bogle long before this conflict gave his counsel not to annex Nepal, on the contrary, recommended Assam to be annexed instead of Nepal or Bhutan. He held,

'Assam itself is an open country of great extent, and by al accounts well cultivated and inhabited ; the road into it either by land or the Brahmaputra lies open.........As the great objection against entering Nepal, etc. arises from the difficulty of keeping open the communications ; so, on the other hand, the easy access to Assam, whether by land or water, invites us to the attempt'.[5]

Here it would not be unwarranted to re-examine the role of Bogle as a commercial envoy. His observation smacks of colonizer and seasoned diplomat who had excellent political foresight. Long before the occupation of Assam its strategic position and valuable natural resources did not escape Bogle's attention. He further observed,

'Assam, as I have already observed yields many valuable articles for exportation. Gold is a considerable article of inland trade...when the restrictions against exportation are taken off, it must give the balance of trade in our favour. Supposing it should not turn out so great an object as I have represented, still it cannot with reason be doubled that it would more than reimburse the Company, by the advantageous terms they would be glad to give us in point of trade, setting all acquisition of territory out of the question ; and I make no doubt but that, a few after our entering Assam, the troops might be paid and provisional with making any demands on the company's treasury'.[6]

Therefore, we have seen that it was not without reason Corn-wallis declined to assist Tibet against Nepal though in the war against Nepal the latter had less possibility to withstand the onslaught of the Company's troops.

Apart from this there was practical difficulty in despatching English troops to Tibet avoiding Nepal.

Cornwallis got into a scrape. He could not find the route. There were then two routes to Tibet from Bengal. One through Nepal and the other through Bhutan. Route through Sikkim was still unknown to the British. The first one i.e. through Nepal was extraneous. The second one hazardous, impassable, hilly upward and downward slope and quite unfit to keep communication and maintain supply from the rear. In addition to this, Tibet's only usefulness to the Company was its passage through which the English could enter into China. But Nepal's hostility would not allow the Company officials to enter into Tibet through Nepal which was passable and easy accessible route.

Again friendship with a distant 'forbidden land', at the cost of Nepal, a country so close to India might have seemed unprofitable to Cornwallis. This English diplomacy or foreign policy envisaged for Tibet was perhaps accurate for that period but appeared to be unmistakably wrong in the subsequent years.

The above reasons were partly true. There must have been another reason—another thought which obviously acted as a very strong one. Cornwallis might have thought that non-interference would please China and as a reward of it she might allow the English merchants to enter into her inland market. But that did not happen. On the contrary, British policy in Tibeto-Nepal war, of which we would discuss later on, muddled the entire situation so much so that the British Government in India was despised by both Nepal and Tibet and the British had to remain inactive in Himalayan affairs for a considerable period of time.

Now let us examine how did this happen? In 1791 the Tibeto-Nepalese war escalated and Tibet felt herself awkward. She maintained no regular army. Hard pressed by

the Nepalese onslaught the Tibetans found no other alternative than to seeking help from China. Immediately China
responded and already prepared Chinese troops under General
Fu-kangun were sent to Tibet to oppose Nepal. Soon Nepal
was driven back across their own frontier and she bought
peace concluding an ignominious treaty on 30 Sept 1792, consenting to pay an annual tribute to the Chinese Emperor and
the full restitution of all the spoils which they carried off.

Unwillingness on the part of Cornwallis to send troops to
Tibet produced some far-reaching consequences creating some
adverse reactions for India, in particular.

In the first place, the British policy begetted an opportunity
for the Chinese authorities in Peking to send troops into
Tibet.

Secondly, Nepal had to bow down to the Chinese might
and henceforth her foreign policy, in regard to India in particular, began to be dictated by China alteast for some
decades.

Thirdly, all the Himalayan States viz., Tibet, Nepal and
Bhutan began treating the British unmistakably unreliable one.

Last but not the least, Tibet was deliberately thrown into
Chinese fold leading to create most unfortunate circumstances
later on, in this Himalayan region.

In fact, the Gorkha invasion on Tibet is a turning point
in the history of political relations between India and China on
which deep researches are needed to be carried out. The
most important aspect of this Tibeto-Nepalese war, which
later on turned into Sino-Nepalese war, is the revelation of
Tibet's political identity. She sought military help from the
British first, leading to disclose her relation with China prov-
ing latter's demand, that Tibet was her vassal state, utterly
falsehood. This has exploded the fallacy. If political status
of Tibet was one of subordinate to China she could not seek
British help. It was only after British refusal she turned her
attention to China and requested to help her, Chinese army
poured into Tibet. China was at that time very much perturbed

and harassed by the Western powers in the opium war. Lured by the Tibetan invitation to assist her which would help to establish her politico-military control over Tibet and to retrieve her lost military prestige in the Opium war, China came forward to drive out the Gorkhas from Lhasa.

In reality, the Tibetans despised the Chinese more than anything. Hence British were their first choice *albeit* they were afraid, of her policy towards the Himalayan region.

Meanwhile, when the war was in progress, Nepal found herself in an awkward position. Finding her in difficulty, British policy once again became active. Lord Cornwallis secretly wrote a letter to the king of Nepal for the supply of British arms in lieu of concluding a trade agreement which would allow the English merchants to carry on trade with Nepal. Jonathan Duncan, the English Resident at Benaras took initiative in this respect and the first treaty of commerce with Nepal was signed on Ist March, 1792.[9]

But no British arms reached Nepal even when she desperately needed it. Nepal was thus pushed to embarassment. After the Sino-Nepal treaty which she compelled to conclude with the former, she had no reason to operate the Anglo-Nepal treaty. So when Kirkpatrick reached Katmandu in September 1792 to revive the treaty all fond-hopes of the East India Company dashed into pieces. The Anglo-Nepal relation reached to its lowest ebb partly due to British failure in supplying Nepal with arms in time of her need which proved the British as an unreliable friend and partly due to her reluctance to develop Anglo-Nepal relations which would have invited China's wrath on her.

D.R. Regmi rightly observes that after this episode, 'It delayed British infiltration into Nepal for at least another fifty years'[10]. British policy towards Nepal proved to be fatal for the English Government in India. But for China it was a bonanza. She found no opposition in Tibet to enlarge her political authority. The deliverer turned into master and earned *locus standi* in internal and external affairs of Tibet imposing a kind of *defacto* sovereignty.

Installing two *Ambans* at Lhasa and an expeditionary force there, China exerted pressure to bring Tibet further under her control. She even tried to influence Panchen Lama by a bribe. The Lama was showered with honour during his visit to Peking and the Chinese Government conspired with him to exercise its greater control in the selection of the Dalai Lama.[11]

Kirkpatrick had to come back empty handed. Being aware fully well that the Tibetans were hostile to the Chinese and had left no stone unturned to drive the Chinese out of their country, neither Cornwallis nor his Government disproved Chinese authority in Tibet exploiting the widespread discontentment among the Tibetans. On the contrary, he chose to support China's claim to exercise her authority over Tibet. In the face of increasing hostility of the Tibetans, the Chinese *Ambans*, became ineffective but in the absence of any foreign help they failed to drive the Chinese army and the *Ambans* out of their country.

With the British evidently supporting the Chinese, the position of Tibet became alarming one. The thirteenth Gyalwa Rimpoche sent an envoy to the Czar of Russia to open negotiations so that effective help could be brought against the Chinese. The Czar was interested and his close attention to Tibet became an alarming to the English of which we would discuss later on

REFERENCES

1. A strange reason benind this invasion has been forwarded by Tibetan source. Panchen or Tashi Lama was invited by the Court of Peking and received with great honour and riches there. Dza Marpa, the brother of Tashi hoped to inherit a portion of riches. Disappointed, he intrigued with the Gorkha king of Nepal who despatched an army to invade Tibet.

2. Diskalkar, D.B. *Macartney papers* JBORS, Vol. 19, p 372

3. *Home Department Consultations*, 22 December, 1788, p. 27.

4. A Lamb, *The China—India Border*.

5. Markham, C.R. (ed), *Narratives of the Mision of George Bogle to Tibet and Journey of Thomas Manning to Lhasa,* Lond. 1876, pp. 57—58.

6. *Ibid,* p. 60

7. *Home Department Consultations, op. cit.*

8. Regmi, D.R. *Medieval Nepal,* pt. I, Calcutta 1965, p. 537.

9. Aitchison, C.U. (Comp.), *A Collection of Treaties, Engagements and Sanands relating to India and Neighbouring countries,* Calcutta 1863, Vol. XIV, p. 56.

10. Regmi, *op. cit.*

Sketch Map showing trade routes between Bengal and Central Tibet in the latter part of the 18th century. [1]

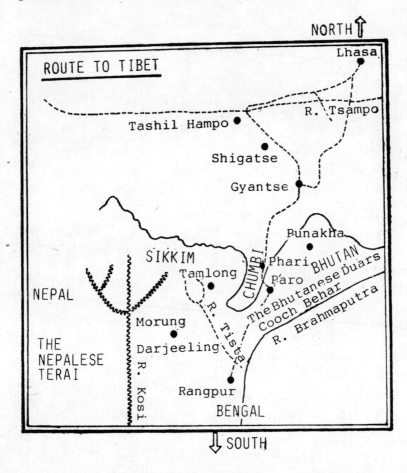

1. Taken from Home Misc., vol. 608, f. 33.

Part III

Decline of Commerce

CHAPTER IV

INDIA-TIBET-CHINA COMMERCE

To take stock of China's political standpoint about Tibet it is essential to look back. Upto the Ming dynasty (1368-1644) China maintained neither cultural nor political relation with Tibet. Even under first quarter of the 18th Century, Tibet remained independent and lay outside the orbit of the Chinese Empire. During this period we find no trace of the theory propagated by the Chinese that Tibet was her vassal state. It was only in 1717 when the Dsungar marauders, a Mongal tribe from Turkestan, invaded Tibet, the contemporary Dalai Lama appealed to the Chinese Emperor, K'ang-Hsi for help. This was quite natural because of two reasons :

Firstly, Tibet maintained no standing army of which mention has been made earlier.

Secondly, except China, there was no country close at hand of Tibet having a powerful army.

However, after a prolonged confrontation, the Chinese army freed Tibet from the marauders in 1720.[1] Now the deliverer turned into master and imposed a kind of *defacto* sovereignty upon Tibet. But the Tibetans, unaccustomed with foreign domination, drove the *Ambans* out of Tibet and massacred the Chinese garrison and threw off Chinese overlordship.[2]

Let us now throw some light on the observations made by Bogle on this issued. He statue that China had established her

supremacy upon Tibet some seventy years before by interven-
ing in the quarrels between two centending parties in Tibet.[3]
The British Government in India, it appears, had accepted this
political situation of Tibet. We have seen earlier, Cornwallis
responded negatively at the prayer of Tibet because of the
pre-conceived idea maintained by the English in India about
China's supremacy over Tibet. The above circumstances
would clear British reluctance in interferring into Tibeto-
Nepalse war which brought about some decisive results and
that we have stated earlier. In addition to this some other
developments took place worth mentioning here. This has been
summed up as follows :

(1) the hold of the Chinese on Tibet was tightened ;

(2) the Indian merchants in Tibet were suspected as agents
of the British, and subsequently driven out of the country.
For the first time in the history of India—Tibet relations, the
Indians seemed to be undesirable in Tibet ;[4]

(3) the Indian pilgrims who often visited the shrines in
Tibet were brought under strict vigilance ;[5]

(4) last but not the least, British interests in the Himalayas
and the reaction of China towards them became a major factor
in eastern Himalayan politics.

The English E.I. Co., however, did not stop altogether
trying to extend its economic interests in China through Tibet.
But it was too late then. The period began from 1791 may be
termed as a turning point in the diplomatic history of India,
Tibet and China. Henceforth, China, attempted to consolidate
her position in Tibet firmly. At the same time Nepal persistently opposed the English in India, to open up the trade
route to Tibet *via* Nepal.

If Nepal did not put obstacles, Captain Kirkpatrick laments
in 1793, 'there is no reason to believe that an extensive trade
might be carried on between Tibet and the British territories
through Nepal, highly beneficial......to the commercial interests
of the English nation'.[6]

Walter Hamilton echoed Kirkpatrick, in the first quarter of
the nineteenth century, when he stated 'If it was not for these
obstacles', i.e. obstacles put forward by Nepal, he held, 'an
extensive traffic might be carried on between Tibet and the

Classics India Publications Mailing List

I would like to be placed on the classics India publications mailing list and to receive the classics India publications catlogue of books and information about future projects.

Name _____

Address _____

Country _____

Book in which
this card was found _____

CLASSICS INDIA PUBLICATIONS

JU-69B, PEETAM PURA,

DELHI - 110 034

(INDIA)

British territories through Nepal'.[7] In this connection, we cannot refrain ourselves from quoting Dr. Francis Buchanan (1814). He stated, 'All attempts to secure commercial advantages by treaty with such a people, I am afraid', Buchanan continued in saying, 'will end in disappointment'.[8]

The observations made above seemed confusing. We know by this time China's hold on Tibet was stronger than before and she would never allow British to be sent in Tibet even if Nepal allowed them passage.

The reasons of Nepal's opposition to British economic penetration has been traced by W.W. Hunter as 'Nepal's eagerness to remain isolate'.[9] He did not go far into the reality. The most reasonable cause has, however, been forwarded by G.C. Sastri in the *Historical Glimpses of Modern Nepal*. He asserts that Bhim Sen Thapa, the Prime Minister of Nepal (1806—37), was afraid of the establishment of British suzerainty in India, where the English originally settled as traders. He, therefore, determined to resist the British trading activities in Nepal and refrained from doing anything which might encourage the British power. He also envisaged a plan to build 'an Asian Front against the growing British Colonialism'.[10]

Bhim sen Thapa was, though not the man of our period, nevertheless his view was universal in Nepal. She looked black at the gradual British establishment of colony in India.

The term colonialism was, most probably, unknown to the Nepali Prime Minister of the time and it appears as an exaggeration of the author himself. Nevertheless, the stubborn resistance offered by the Prime Minister and the maintainance of the anti-British policy for a longer period draws our attention.

India had no direct territorial link with China. The old overland trade route usually known as 'silk route,' went northeast to Kashgar and thence to Succur, Singanfu, Nanking and Canton in China. Obtaining the *Dewani* of Bengal *Subah*[11] in 1765 the English East India Company for the first time came contact with Bhutan, a Himalayan State. We have seen the Company had been engaged in armed conflict with Bhutan and this was ended by the mediation of the Tashi Lama of Tibet offering golden opportunity to satisfy Company's cherished desire of opening up of China's market through Tibet. The provision of the treaty concluded with Bhutan allowed her merchants to carry on trade with Bengal.

Tibet has direct territorial link with China and this has made the situation complex for India. Knowledge in Tibetan and Chinese languages and access into documents of both countries are essential to examine their mutual relation, otherwise any observation would be incomplete and partial. Nevertheless, I have attempted to throw some light on the mutual relation among India-Tibet and China depending mainly on the documents translated into English because we can not afford any more delay to clear some misconceptions which seem to be the root of dissension between India and China in particular, and without the clearance of which normalization of relation is impossible. Apparently, the present relation between India and China appears to be peaceful. Nevertheless, China regarded India's offer to normalise the situation as a hoax. Her approach to border problem is unintelligible to India. The Chinese have reiterated their claim to Arunachal regularly, for the record on most occasions, such as during the Delhi Asiad and in a practical way now by building installations at Wangdong in the Sumdorong Chu Valley.

To deal with China's obstinate unilateral demand, India should have a clear conception about her stand as well as China's historical position in the Himalayan region. With this view, I have examined China's real position and relation in and with Himalayan states particularly Tibet. Relation depends on the mentality of individual which further grows out of experience that one gathers from history. History may be interpreted by individual attitude but impartial treatment is an indispensable condition for an historian. Therefore, to review the relation between India and China, it is necessary to look back and throw light on China's unilateral demand on Tibet as her vassal state.

Regarding the selection of the Dalai Lama, China propagated that it was their Emperor who enjoyed the authority of selecting the Dalai Lama. The subject bristles with problems and controversies. Information, however, to deal with the subject, is extremely scanty. In fact, the Fourth Dalai Lama,

Yoten Gyatso, was a Mongol. The Dalai Lamas were originally installed in authority in Tibet by the Mongols.

We have seen earlier that China under Ming dynasty maintained no diplomatic connection with Tibet upto 1644. Chinese merchants were the only linkmen between Tibet and China. If we trace the history of Tibet from thirteenth century onwards, it would be found that Kublai Khan, the Emperor of China, 'divided Tibet into provinces, and gave the title of king to the Lama of Lhasa'. Yonglo, the king of Ming dynasty of China, again conferred on Eight Lama of Lhasa, the title of king in 1373 and the title was refused. The Chinese historians described the event as the imposition of Chinese sovereignty on Tibet.[12]

But this is entirely an untenable argument. The Lamas accepted the title but ignored to abide by the decision of Chinese authorities in matters of Tibetan administration. As a result a series of crisis corpped up in Tibet against the elder brotherly attitude of China.[13]

Towards the end of fourteenth century, the Tibetan religious reformer Tsong Kapa founded the Yellow (or Gelukpa) Sect and laid the foundations for that system of incarnate Lamas which has characterised Tibetan Government ever since. The post of the Dalai Lima was created by him.

There is a second version. In 1426 these Lamas took the title of Grand Lama and the Lama of Lhasa took the distinguishing authority to select the Dalai Lama. But the Chinese interference in the selection of the Dalai Lama proved to be a great source of danger to the integrity and sovereignty of Tibet. The favourite diplomacy, Chinese authority usually applied was to create division among the members of the Grand Lama.[14] This was made possible as a result of dissension among the members of the Grand Lama. There is yet another version. Typa Lama was chosen by the great Tibetan religious reformer Tsong-ka-pa as the Dalai Lama.[16]

Therefore, it cannot altogether be said that the Chinese enjoyed exclusive authority in matters of selection of the Dalai Lama and thereby infringed upon the sovereignty of Tibet.

Hence, it is difficult to draw a definite conclusion as to the correctness of conflicting theories behind the creation of

sovereign authority in Tibet. But the Chinese interference in
Tibet by and by grew large. The Resident Political Agent of
China was appointed in Lhasa in 1720. At last in 1749,
Tibetan insurrection against the Resident Political Agent of
China broke out which ended in Lobsong Kalsang, the Sixth
Dalai Lama being established at Lhasa and the Chinese Am-
ban dirven out. The Sixth Dalai died in 1758.[17]

Obviously Chinese influence on Tibet, as a result of this
revolt, decreased to a great extent but could not be wiped
out totally because of its comparatively large and better military power. China deployed her army within quick striking
distance of the border. Since then until 1790 China could not
extend or spread any political influence on Tibet. It is the invasion of Nepal which enabled them to re-enter into Tibet.
The military pressure compelled Tibet again to accept two
Chinese Political agents or *Ambans* to be posted in the Court
of Lhasa.[18] But Chinese presence in Tibet was not at all
peaceful. The Tibetans rose again and again to battle against
Chinese machinations in Tibet.[19]

This disturbing circumstances in Tibet hindered India's
trading possibility with that country. Bogle actually could not
proceed to Lhasa due to objection raised by general public of
Tibet.[20] He had to come back from Tashil Humpo.[21] But
Tashi Lama informed Bogle that Chinese Political Agent
opposed to Bogle's entry. Hence the Lama discouraged Bogle
to go to Lhasa.[22] But Chinese opposition to Bogle is most
probably fictitious, because it was the Tibetan people who not
only objected to going to Lhasa but also they opposed to Bogle's
long staying in Tibet.[23] Tashi Lama also expressed his feelings
to Bogle saying that in future it would be desirable if the
Company sent Indian Hindu merchants to Tibet and not the
English.[24]

From the above observations it can be inferred that the
Tibetans suspected the English so much so that they could
not even tolerate single Englishman and disallowed him to
enter into Lhasa.[25]

When Bogle met the Lama, the latter expressed his concern
saying that the English, he heard, were very much 'fond of war
and conquest' and so he was unable 'to admit any Firingis into

the country'.[26]   Tashi Lama's observations about the English
are stupendous and true to the point.   He was equally aware
of British commercial activities which tended to spread imperialistic aggression particularly in the Asian countries.

Tashi Lama also stated that inspite of opposition offered by
Gesub Rimpoche, the Tibetan agent for China, the Lama made
arrangement for Bogle's arrival.[27]   The two Deputies of the
Dalai Lama came to meet Bogle and to learn his motive.[28]
Bogle disclosed his motive stating that the English Company
sought to establish commercial relation with Tibet.   The response from the Lhasa representatives was neither positive nor
altogether negative.   Shrwedly they mentioned that it entirely
depended on Gesusb Rimpoche and the latter would try to
help him. They however, did not stop mentioning that
Rimpoche's power was limited because Tibet was a vassal
state of China.[29]

This is entirely an imaginary statement. There was a rivalry
between Tashi Lama and Rimpoche. The latter consults him
'as seldom as possible' in matters of administration. 'The
grand object of Gesub's politics is to secure the administration
to himself and afterwards to his nephews'. To achieve his
success, he maintained a very good relation with China and the
latter always tried to find fault with the Tibetans and did not
hesitate to punish them.   In addition to t his China always
interferred into the internal affairs of Tibet and the latter had
to accept it because of her lack of military power. These
nefarious activities of China were not carried on, however, by
her directly, but through her obsequious agent like Rimpoche.

In this connection, it is hardly necessary to recall Peking's
armed assistance to Tibet to rescue her from Gorkha invasion
and for which Peking authorities demanded her allegiance to
them. It was equally essential for Tibet to maintain friendly
relation with China to save herself from foreign aggression.
Peking always tended to exploit this situation. It is not
known whether any agreement was concluded between them by
which Tibet accepted Peking's sovereignty on her. Most
probably this was not done. If this would have been done
Chinese brigades were not required to plunge into Tibet in
1950.

However, in course of his discussion with the Tashi Lama, Bogle apprised him that the Lhasa Deputies informed that Rimpoche would try to help him. Most probably, the offer was made to refrain Bogle from accepting any assistance from Tashi Lama. On the contrary, the Lama informed Bogle that obstacles to his 'journey arose chiefly from Gesub Rimpoche' of Lhasa. Tashi Lama showed Bogle a letter, written in Tibetan language, in which, the Lama stated, that Rimpoche requested him, 'to find some methods of sending' Bogle 'back, either on account of violence of the small pox or on any other pretence'[30]

The above incident evidently clears the situation. At first Rimpoche wanted to thwart Bogle's entrance into Tibet and the Tashi Lama was in favour of Bogle's arrival. This was because Rimpoche might have thought the alliance between Tashi Lama and the English might endanger his position.

Rimpoche knew very well that the English were very powerful and Tashi Lama favoured them. So he had recourse to two methods :

Firstly, he tried to stop Bogle's entrance into Tibet.

Secondly, when he found his first measure proved useless, he sent his Deputies to Bogle informing him that he needed no help from Tashi Lama. On the contrary, he was ready to assist him.

To secure Bogle's safety, Tashi Lama wrote Taranath Lama, who was then at Peking, informing him of Bogle's arrival. Most probably this was done to win the support of Taranath against Rimpoche. He wrote that 'the English are new masters of Bengal.........that the English allow every one to follow his own religion unmolested.........' Evidently he pleaded for the English.

Bogle fervidly hoped to foster Anglo-Tibet friendly relations which Tashi Lama was told would prevent any further Gorkha attack on Tibet.[31] But Tashi Lama did not perhaps forget previous refusal of the English. He also knew the fate of India, where augmentation of British influence led to its conquest. Again grant of any commercial privilege to the English in Tibet would embitter his relation with China, especially when the possibility of further Gorkha invasion had not yet been eliminated.

The Lhasa Deputies asked Bogle to leave Tibet as soon as possible and denied to make an arrangement of sending any letter to Peking containing the request of allowing the English to carry on trade with China. Being surprised Bogle wrote 'I confess, I was much struck with the answer'.[32] If Bogle would not have the preconceived idea of China's supremacy on Tibet, he had nothing to be surprised. China was a foreign country to Tibet and there was no justification of carrying English letter to China.

Bogle complained all about this to Tashi Lama and asked the reason of this. Tashi had no answer because he himself informed Bogle that Tibet was a vassal state of China. Therefore, to pacify him Tashi wrote a letter to Lhasa authorities requesting 'in the name of the Governor my master, that you will allow merchants to trade between this country (Tibet) and Bengal'.[33]

The peculiarity of this letter is to be noted. Tashi did not ask the Lhasa authorities to allow the English merchants, but the merchants of Bengal. This proves that in spite of friendly relations between Bogle and Tashi, the latter was unwilling to trust the English.

However, the answer to the above letter did never come. A close investigation into the documents helps us to know the reason. The Gorkha king wrote both Tashi Lama and Rimpoche threatening them to cut off relation with the English and turned Bogle out of Tibet immediately otherwise, they would invade Tibet.[34]

This letter of the Gorkha king raises some pertinent questions. Firstly, after the defeat by China in 1791 the latter propagated that the Gorkha king concluded an ignominious treaty with her consenting to pay an indemnity and yearly tribute. But how far this is true is not known to us. If it was so, the Gorkha King did not dare to think for a further invasion against Tibet. Secondly, if Tibet would have been a vassal state of China, then threatening should have come from her. Thirdly, throughout the period of English activities in Tibet we do not find any reference which can prove that China urged or threatened Tibet to stop English activities there, particularly when China strongly opposed the English commercial activities in her main land.

We have seen China under Ming dynasty had no contact with Tibet. The Manchu dynasty was founded by Shun Che in 1651. This dynasty had produced two really powerful Emperors Kang-hi and Kien Lung. The former reigned from 1662 to 1723 while the latter from 1763-1796. It was in 1720 under the Emperor Kanghi, China opened diplomatic relations with Tibet sending diplomatic representatives to be posted at Lhasa.[35]

The Gorkha expedition further enabled China to superimpose her political authorities over the Dalai Lama curtailing some of his political powers. It has already been mentioned that a Chinese army had also been stationed in Tibet.

Several restrictions were imposed on the Indian Buddhists visiting Tibetan monsteries. As a result, Indo-Tibet religious and cultural relations were also suspended. India-China political relations since then created an atmosphere of future uneasiness. Tibet, on her part, tried to overthrow Chinese supremacy over her more than once. The Chinese *Ambans* were expelled and army massacred. But new troops having modern weapons were brought in to put down the mutiny. Help neither moral nor military came from India.

Despite this it is not surprising that the British Government in India neither protested against the Chinese activities in Tibet nor did anything to check their illegal intrusion. This is most probably due to the fact that the British knew very well that their activities in India were illegal so they had no moral justification to oppose the Chinese in Tibet. Moreover, this would have endangered their commercial base at Canton.

British policy in Tibet was one of appeasement The Nepal-Tibet war offered the English golden opportunity and their participation in favour of any country either Nepal or Tibet, would have given them a commanding position in the

Himalayan region and Chinese settlements in Tibet could not be eastablished without the consent of the English, which China enjoyed now.

Considering all these pros and cons we can draw this conclusion that British diplomacy in the Himalayan region totally failed. Alstair Lamb rightly denounced British diplomacy for her non-intervention policy in Tibet and observed 'British dipolmacy was a failure'.[36] India could have been in an advantageous position, if British could gain a foot-hold in Tibet. She could have been relieved of yellow-phobia and the English did not need Younghusband expedition in 1904.

There was another side. China's invading army came within twenty miles of Katmandu and they could easily occupy some areas of Nepal, but did not and retired only accepting annual tribute to be paid to the Emperor of China and the full restitution of all the spoils which they carried off.[37]

By this action they not only earned Nepal's gratitude but successfully helped forming an impression among the Tibetans that the British imperialists in India encouraged Nepal to invade Tibet.

China devised a plan of the selection of the Dalai Lama through lottery from several candidates. The names of which would be placed in a golden urn and the final selection was to be made by the Chinese representatives posted at Lhasa who drew out one name. Tibet denied to accept the system and therefore it could not last long.

When Kirkpatrick reached Kathmandu in 1793, he found a complete change in the situation of this Himalayan state. The Chinese position in Tibet brought about an alteration in the Balance of Power. Kirkpatrick observed, if, 'the Chinese were to establish themselves permanently in our neighbourhood, the border incidents always intensify to such a situation, would be but too liable to disturb, more or less, the commercial relation subsisting between them and the East India Company in another part of Asia.'[38]

At this stage Lord Macartney's embassy[39] was to leave for Peking by sea from London. Hence Kirkpatrick argued that this subject, i.e. British relation with Tibet, of 'sufficient gravity' was to be included in the agenda of Macartney's discussion with the Chinese Emperor.[40]   Macartney who was then on his way to meet the Emperor at Jehol was, however, surprised when he heard that the Chinese Emperor was very much angry at the way in which the British helped Nepal's war activities against China. His reaction at this was very tense.

Macartney remarked'.........that the thing was impossible and that I could take it upon me to contradict it in the most decisive manner'.[41]

In fact, this impression of the Chinese was, wholly responsible for the failure of Macartney's Mission to China. The distrust of the Chinese as to the nature of British role in the recent Himalayan crisis (1788-91) made the latter a stunch enemy of Nepal, Tibet and China.

Again, the increased power of China so close to the borders of British India posed a grave threat for future. Let us see what Sir Staunton observed in this connection. He put it '... should an interference take place in future, on the part of His imperial, the dissensions which frequently arise between the princes possessing the countries lying along the eastern limits of Hindostan,.........there may be occasion for mutual discussion between the British and Chinese Governments and so slight precaution may be necessary on their parts to avoid being involved in, the quarrels of their respective dependents or allies'.

Staunton believed that danger was unavoidable on the both frontiers of Assam and the Himalayas.[42] China's illegal and arbitrary demand on Arunachal Pradesh reminds us that warning at last becoming true. Macartney desired to send another mission to Peking. It was very much essential because he thought that the Chinese suspicion on the role of British policy in the Himalayas should be removed. Otherwise the very possessions of the British in India would be threatened sooner or later.

But nothing was done from British side except correspondence.[43] British policy in Tibet remained inactive until 1904.

The door of Tibet was closed to British India and in the absence of reliable information, the problem became a difficult one. From 1791 China's policy in Tibet became one of continuous intervention in its internal affairs.[44]

W.W. Hunter, the British historian, therefore very carefully avoided the real causes of the failure of British diplomacy in Tibet. Nepal's apathy towards British in India has been described by him as her 'eagerness to remain isolate'.[45]

But this is a multitude of lies. In fact, British attempt to extend their political influence in India and beyond, expedition to Bhutan and reluctance to help Nepal in her extreme need in spite of their promise frightened Nepal so much so that she did not dare to negotiate with the English.

REFERENCES

1. L. Petech, *China and Tibet in the Early Eighteenth Century* (Leyden, 1950), Ch. 111-IV.

2. Charles Dell, *Tibet, Past and Present*, pp. 61-62.

3. Bogle, Ch. XIV, P. 130,

4. Younghusband, *Op. cit.*, p. 31.

5. *Ibid.*

6. Kirkpatrick *Op. Cit.*, P. 204.

7. Walter Hamilton, *East India Gazetteer*, (Lond. 1827) p. 607.

8. Francis Buchanan, *An Account of the District of Purnea in* 1809-10, p.556.

9. W.W. Hunter, *The Life Brain Houghton Hodgson*, (Lond. 1896), p. 114.

10. G.C. Sastri, *Historical Glimpses of modern Nepal* (Kathmandu, n.d. pp. 25 ; Jahar Sen, *Op. Cit*, p-26.

11. *Subah* means a provinice comprising of Bengal, Bihar and Orissa then.

12. Bogle, *Op. Cit.*, p. 10

13. At least on two occasions in 1720 and in 1749 insurrections against the Chinese broke out. Bogle, *Op. Cit.*, p. 130.

14. The rift was created successfully by the Chinese between Tashi Lama and Gesub Rimpoche is the best illustration. For further discussion see I. Desideri, *An Account of Tibet* ed. by F de Fillippi, Lond. 1932 ; W.W. Rockhill, *The Dalai Lamas and their relations with the Manchu Emperors of China.*

15. For details see Sir C. Dell, *Op. Cit.* ; S. Cammann, *Op. Cit ,*

16. See S. Cammann.

17. Bogle, *Op. Cit.*, P. 130.

18. *H.M.* Vol. 219, pp. 384-85.

19. Mentioned previously.

20. Bogle, *Op. Cit.*, p. 162. The Tibetans in general, were not in favour of the Europeans and English in particular. According to a Tibetan proverb, the British are the road makers of Tibet, i.e., They have shown to others the path leading to Lhasa.

21. *Ibid.*, p. 167.

22. *Ibid.*, p. 162.

23. *Ibid.*

24. *Ibid.*

25. Younghusband, p. 38

26. Bogle, *Op. Cit.*, p. 131

27. *Ibid.* He also obstructed the journey of Captain Turner.

28. *H.M..* Vol. 219, p. 373.

29. Bogle, Op. Cit., p. 161.

30. *Ibid.*, p. 131

31. *H.M.*, Vol. 219, p. 373.

32. Bogle, *Op.Cit.*, p. 161.

33. *Ibid.*

34. *Ibid.* Tashi Lama mentioned 'while the administration is in Gesub's hands (Gesub Rinpoche) he and the Amban (Chinese Resident Officials) are excessive jealous of foreigners coming into the country, so much so that he stopped the admission of a *Vakil* from the king of Assam'.

    Ibid, p. 155

    Rimpoche is an horific term given to revered teachers or incarnate Lamas. it means 'precious one'.

35. *Ibid*, p. V.

36. Alstair Lamb, *Britatin and Chinese Central Asia, The Road to Lhasa*, 1767 to 1905 (I.O.L, London), p.22 (Lond. 1960).

37. D.R. Regmi, *Modern Nepal* (Cal. 1961), p. 160.

38. Krikpatrick, *Op.Cit.*, pp. 371-9.

39. J. Barrow, *Some Accounts of the Public Life and a Selection of the unpublished writings of the Earl of Macartney*, Vol. II pp 3-4 (I.O.L, London), Lond. 1807.

40. Kirkpatrick, *Op.Cit.*, p. 372.

41. J. Barrow, *Op.Cit.*

42. Sir G. Bart Staunton, *An Authentic Account of an Embassy from Great Britain to the Emperor of China*, Vol. II (I O L, London), pp. 227-8, Lond. 1797.

43. P. Auber, *China : an outline of its Government, Laws and Policy* (IOL, London), p. 129 Lond. 1834.

44. At their insistence, Tibetan authorities closed their country to Indian merchants. The selection of the Dalai Lama depended on China's choice.

45. Extracted from G.C. Shastri, *Op.Cit.* p. 38.

CHAPTER V

I

TRADE AND POLITICS

In 18th Century Tibet was on the threshold of disaster due to the presence of Russia and China in Central Asia. Both cherished the same object of promoting their politico-economic interests in Tibet.

In this discussion we have tried to concentrate our attention on the Russian activities and influence that she tried to enhance in Tibet and which made apprehensive both China and the British in India. Apprehending Russian assault on her, China was so much distrubed that she could not even pose a threat to the British expansion towards N.E. India, on the contrary, she sought help from the Tibetans to rescue her from Russian design against her, of which we would discuss elaborately later on. The region both north-east and north-west of India which were also threatened by Russian advance and her influence that she tried to exert on Tibet became a matter of concern to the Government of the English East India Company during the period of our discussion.

Therefore, it became increasingly essential for the British imperialists in India to take precaution in order to oppose the

Russian threat. So a policy, namely the Forward Policy was taken up by the English rulers in India. On the one hand, they wanted to destroy Russo-Tibetan commercial and diplomatic relations, while on the other, they wanted to construct the foundation of Anglo-Tibet diplomatic as well as commericial relations anew. With this object in view we would try to throw light on the following aspects :

    (i)   Russo-Tibetan Commercial Relations ;

    (ii) Russo-Tibetan Diplomatic Relations ;

    (iii) British reactions to Russian progress ;

    (iv) India-Central Asian Trade.

But before we go into the details some light is also to be thrown on the development of Russian interests in Central Asia.

Russia's advance towards Sinkiang and Tibet was first noticed in 1580 when a Cossack brigand conquered the tribes to the east of the Urals. Her mercantile marine was also gathered at the ports of China, when other European maritime nations were busy attempting to open the door of China to foreign intercourse. The territory to the East of the Urals was incorporated into Russia. Lake Baikal was reached in 165!. But her move towards Manchuria and attempt to occupy the region was however thwarted by the Manchus steadily. Samarkhand and Bokhara were annexed in 1868 and Tashkhant in 1885.[1]

(i) Russo-Tibetan Commercial Relations.

Ample references to the presence of Russian merchants in Tibet are available in the English documents during the period of our discussion. In this connection, I express my inability to look into Tibetan and Russian documents which are beyond my access due to various reasons.

Samuel Turner, the English East India Company's representative in Tibet, apprised us in 1782 that the Regent and Ministers of Tibet told him that Russia had been making many overtures to extend her commerce to the internal parts of Tibet.[2] Though the disinclination of the Tibetans, observed Turner, discouraged the Russian merchants to try to make commercial contact with Tibet, the Russians often came and traded with her[3] and the Tibetans allowed them to do so. This appears that Turner's observation is not wholly true.

The bulk of Russo-Tibetan trade was carried on by the Kalmukhs who lived in the Eastern Turkestan and on the banks of the lower Volga. They had embraced the Lama religion and regarded the Dalai Lama as their spiritual leader. Every year they came to Tibet, to pay their devotions at the Lama's shrines, bringing their camels loaded with furs and other Siberian goods......'[4] The Kalmukhs brought to Tibet red and black Russian leather hides, yaktails, some camels, furs, bastered pearls[5] and silver which they bartared for broad cloths, amber beads, spices and gold.[6]

But this trade sustained set back when the Kalmukhs went to China for good leaving their hearth and home in Russia. Oppressed by Russian tyranny the Kalmukhs had left Russia in 1771 and after suffering fearful hardships they crossed Kirkhiz steeps and reached Chinese territory with their number reduced from 6,00,000 to 2,50,000. Kien Lung, the Emperor of China, provided for them with princely munificance, and they settled on the banks of the Illy.[7] This incident obviously made Sino-Russian relations inconstant.

Besides the Kalmukhs there were other Russian merchants who carried on trade with Tibet. Importing peltry from Canada, finer variety of cotton, woolen cloths, glassware and hardware from England they sold those in the markets of China.[8] Bulk of these commodities were re-sold in Tibet by the Chinese merchants. Besides, the Rulssians sold products of Siberia 'consist of furs, red and black, Bulgar hides, cowtails, some dromedaries, bastard pearls and silver' in Tibet in lieu of Tibetan 'broad cloth, coral and amber beads, spices and gold'.[9]

(ii) Russo-Tibetan Diplomatic Relations

As regards to the diplomatic relations between Russia and Tibet and so far my opportunity of looking into documents in English language, I have not found any direct reference to any political or diplomatic agreement between the countries in order to develop their mutual relations. Nevertheless, there is no doubt that trading prospects of Tibet must have pushed Russia to turn her attention towards this state. This is not at all unusual because it is a general practice of each and every country to tend to establish commercial relation with other countries where there is possibility of lucrative commercial transactions.

Tibet had better prospects in trade and commerce because of her vulnerable position. India and Nepal enriched with natural and agricultural resources lying on her one flank, while China and Russia on the others. Contact with Tibet means the possibility of acquiring commodities of all these regions which had extensive markets in the other three countries.

Considering the vulnerability of Tibet it is not at all surprising where Russia would try to make inroads by any means and here there lies the possibility of establishing diplomatic relations.

The reference to Russia's diplomatic relation with Tibet is known to us for the first time when the Tashi Lama who is more familiar as Panchen Lama of Tibet made known to George Bogle,[10] the first representative of the English East India Company in Tibet in 1774, his concern about a quarrel between the Russians and the Chinese over some Tartar tribe. He maintained further that in the dispute he was requested by the Chinese Emperor to mediate between two countries to normalise the situation. In the event mentioned above two aspects are visible.

In the first place, the Chinese Emperor believed that there was a very cordial relations between Russia and Tibet.

Secondly, a separate relation on state level with a sovereign country like Russia makes it clear that Tibet enjoyed a separate entity till then and as a representative of soverign ruler, Panchen Lama[11] was requested by the Chinese Emperor to exert his influence over the Russian Emperor. This version also explodes the theory that China enjoyed some kind of political control on Tibet.

The Lama however, believed thet the war between China and Russia was inevitable. He, therefore, predicted that the

Russians had not yet begun hostilities, but he imagined they would soon go to war about it.[12]

But Bogle thought otherwise. Analysing the contemporary situation, he came to the conclusion that at this stage the Russians had no capacity to wage war against China. Admirably Bogle was correct in his prediction. His impression was that as the Russians 'were engaged in a very heavy war with the Turks, which I was uncertain whether they yet finished......' Therefore, he thought that the Russians 'would hardly think of entering into another with the Chinese, and encountering two such powerful neighbours at the same time'.[13]

The Lama might have tried to settle the dispute between China and Russia but was of no avail because 'the Russians had since sent four ambassadors to China', the Lama apprised Bogle 'to demand their vassals, whom the emperor had imprisoned.........'[14]

Dorjieff's[15] pamphlet of later years make us believe that there was some kind of close link between Tibet and Russia from very olden times. In the pamphlet he had shown that the Czar was an incarnation of one of the founders of Lamaism, and the Tibetans believed that the Czar would sooner or later subdue the whole world and found a gigantic Buddhist Empire.[16] Dorjieff's visit in 1900 to Tibet has been described by Kawaguchi, the well known Jampanese traveller, as a diplomatic mission. According to him, Dorjieff, on behalf of the Czar, despatched Russian firearms to the Tibetans.[17]

Though Dorjieff's visit and activities in Tibet were of later years and are not coming within the purview of our discussion at present, it is referred here only to show that an understanding between this two countries was most probably of a long standing. Lack of evidence of Tibet's politico-economic relation with other countries of 17th, 18th and 19th centuries has made our task formidable to cross check the remarks made in the later years.

The famous leader of the Young husband Expedition in Tibet in 1904, Sir Francis Younghusband has written a monumental volume *India and Tibet* after his expedition which was published from London in 1910. In the book he has related the back ground of the expedition describing some very important fragmentary history of Tibet since English East India Company's debut to open the door of Tibet for the English merchants. References to Dorjieff and Kawaguchi are available in this volume. Though incomplete, and lack of source wherefrom he collected his evidence the volume itself presented a lot of important infomation regarding Tibet.

British Reaction to Russian Progress

The Russo-Chinese commercial relations which began from very earlier period further developed after the Treaty of Nerchinsk (August 27, 1689) in order to the establishment of a common frontier and commercial transaction between two countries[18] which ensued a better politico-economic relation between them. At the same time the maritime nations of Europe were insisting on the opening of China to foreign intercourse. But the development of Russo-Chinese relations must have hindered British commercial interests in China. Russia's commercial link with Tibet was also detested by the British in India.

So the English East India Company resorted to a plan for driving the Russians out from this region so that she could no longer pose any threat to British commercial interests both in Tibet and in China.

The scheme prepared in this connection, by Brian Hughton Hodgson is very much interesting and novel in many respects and therefore, worthy to relate here. Hodgson was appointed as Company's Assistant Resident in Nepal, and engaged himself from 1831 for at least twenty years with a view to capturing Trans-Himalayan trade across Tibet to China. His report on this trade has been described as 'Land mark' in the history of Trans-Himalayan trade during our period of discussion.

According to Hodgson, it would not altogether be difficult task for the English in India to drive the Russian out because the trade-route from St. Petersburg to Peking was not less than 5000 kilometre and a hazardous one, whereas the route from Calcutta to Peking is only 2,000 K.M. The water—passage

from St. Petersburg to Peking took three years and the land
route one whole year. On the other hand, short distance between
Calcutta and Peking needed less time to cover it. Hodgson
advocated to introduce British trade with China through this
route. At the end of which the British merchants would enter
into Setchuan, the commercial province of China on the
Yangtze and Hoangho, where they could sell Indian and
European products and buy Chinese one especially tea and
silk only to sell in Tibet and India.

   Though this trade was to be carried on by the Indian and
Nepali merchants, Hodgson observes, they would play no
other role than carriers of goods only of the English East India
Company. Hodgson frankly confessed 'Let the native merchants
of Calcutta and Nepal' to be only carrier of merchandise to
Setchuan 'whilst we (the English merchants) though not the
immediate mover shall yet reap the great advantage of it'[19]
obviously a dirty design cherished by the English.

   So, if Britain could penetrate into Trans-Himalayan as well
as China trade through Tibet, Hodgson remarks, not only the
Russians could easily be replaced in their profitable trade
with China but also Russian menace to British empire could
be warded off once for all. This was not all. The Chinese
demand for Indian goods can also be meted out and the Tibetan
demand for Chinese satins, silks and velvets could be replaced
by British broad clothes and velvets.[20]

   Now the British attempt to establish politico-economic
relation with Tibet found to be a difficult one. To materialize
Hodgson's proposal, Tibet's effective assistance was essential.
But the Company authorities were not allowed by the Tibetan
hierarchy to open any such negotiation. The reason behind
this is not found in any contemporary document except Bogle's
narrative where he attributed the motive of the Tibetans to
remain aloof from the British. According to him the Tibetans
were afraid of British territorial expansion towards north-
eastern India. This is corroborated by the sayings of Tashi
Lama during his interview with George Bogle in 1775. The

Lama said that many Tibetans had advised him against receiving an Englishman. He continued further that 'I had heard
also much of the power of the Firingies : that the Company
(English East India Company) was like a great king, and fond
of war and conquest, and as my business and that of my
people is to pray to God, I was afraid to admit any Firingies
into the country.'[21]

Another plausible reason can be drawn from Tibet's earlier
attempt to seek the favour of the English East India Company
during Gorkha's Tibet expedition which bore no fruit and this
must have cautioned them about English friendship. Though
help of the English was very much essential to the Tibetans at
least during this period because the Chinese attempt to extend
her authority on Tibet becoming more and more forceful and
the help of the British military power could have enabled them
to drive the Chinese out of Tibet, it was equally difficult
for the Tibetans to compel British force vacate Tibet after
accomplishing the mission. Therefore, it appears to us that
the Tibetans might have thought that the known enemy i.e. the
Chinese, was better than the unknown one i.e. the English.

The Tibetans did not want the Chinese as their master while
at the same time, they showed themselves to the British as a
subject of China and Tibet was a vassal state as such.[22] The
diplomacy practised by them in this way later on, proved to
be suicidal for them as well. On the one hand, the English
stopped trying to establish any diplomatic or commercial relation with Tibet apprehending that this might lead them to a
confrontation with China, which the Company disliked, while
on the other, Tibet could not raise her voice when actually
China prompted to gobble her.

II

INDIA-CENTRAL ASIAN TRADE

Some Russian documents of 18th century throw wholly new light on commercial and financial activities of Indian merchants as well as on Russian trade relations with India. These documents show that some Indian merchants were active in Central Asian states of Russia for a fairly long period. A list of Indian merchants are given below who lived and traded in Central Asian states.

Sukhananda	for 25 years	(1735-60)
Magandas (Sukhananda's nephew)	for 38 years	(1760-98)
Nabagi (? Nabhaji)	for 32 years	(1730-62)
Ambu Ram	for 17 years	(1706-23)
Kasi Ram	for 13 years	(1742-52)
Shantu (? Shantu Ram)	for 4 years	(1745-49)

Besides them there were Danismand Khan and Suvan (Subhan) who lived for one year in 1706[23] and still there were others whose name could not be known because of lack of record.

Astrakhan, on the Caspian sea, was the principal trading centre where the merchants of different nations assembled together, accommodated themselves in particular areas, and even enjoyed Russian citizenship, i.e. they enjoyed all the rights and privileges usually granted to the inhabitants. Even the prayer of

Indian merchants for the right to trade free from exactions, in all cities and towns of Russia was granted in 1750.

They explored the possibilities of trade throughout the length and breadth of Russia. They moved from Astrakhan to Moscow and then to Petersburg and back to Astrakhan. The Indian merchants even petitioned Tzar Peter I in 1723 for permission to travel to China through Russian territory.[24]

The activities of Indian merchants were widespread. They engaged themselves in property transactions, viz. sale of land, purchase of farm buildings, buy and sale of war prisoners, sale of Indian gold pieces. There are again, abundant references to loans given by Indian merchants to the Russians, and trading contracts between them in Central Asian Khanates such as Khiva, Bokhara and Astrakhan. The Indians engaged local workmen and residents as their salesmen. As a result legal complications cropped up over the issue like wages and others which throw sufficient light on the contemporary Russian legal system.[25]

Of the various trade-routes for direct Russo-India trade the followings can be summed up :

(a) Over land

  (i) *Via* Afghanistan to Central Asian Khanates ;

  (ii) *Via* Persia. Two treaties were concluded between Russia and Persia. One for security of Russian merchants going to India, and the other in 1732 for free trade in Persia.

(b) Sea-route

  (i) North-sea route.

  (ii) The Arctic and Pacific Ocean route was also considered, sending Russian naval officers on English ships (1763).

There were as many as seven proposals submitted to establish a company in Russia for trade with India :

  (i) An Englishman submitted his proposal to the Empress Anna Ivanavna (1740).

    (ii) by an another Englishman in 1794 ;

   (iii) by a French Marshall in 1796 ;

   (iv) by a Russian with the support of Imam of Oman 1799;

    (v) by a Dutchman to the Board of Trade in 1762-3 ;

   (vi) by a member of the Collegium of Foreign Affairs in 1783 ;

  (vii) by a vice-Governor of Astrakhan in 1792.[26]

From the above discussion we can come to the conclusion that the Indian merchants took part in both foreign and inland trade of Central Asia. But by 1778 restrictions were imposed on Indian merchants limiting the period of their residence. In all probability, this restriction might have been the upshot of British attempt of economic penetration towards Tibet. The Indians, subjects of the English East India Company, ceased to exist as dependable to the Russians. Though there is no direct reference to the reason behind Russian's aversion to Indian merchants, considering the contemporary events narrated above it is not surprising that the Russian administration might have found Indian merchants secretly acting on behalf of the British Intelligence Department. The doubt is further enhanced by the generous encouragement given to the Indian merchants by the Government of English East India Company in India for sending them to Russia for trading and living.

Besides these places, Eastern Turkistan is also to be included in the list of India's foreign trading contacts. Its common frontier with China, Russia and India made her an important centre of trade. Yarkand and Khotan, the two important places of the country from where important trade was conducted. Eastern Turkistan consisted mainly of three district of Semipalantinsk, Syr Dariya and Zarafshan. The country was rich in natural resources. Gold, silver, silk and wool were available abundantly. China annexed this country in the middle of the eithteenth century. Alarmed by the Russian presence in the door step Yakoob Beg, a Kokandi adventurer, — captured the country in 1863, driving the Chinese out and to keep his position secured he wanted to have a friendship with British India.

But the British administration failed to take any initiative in this respect because of the presence of Russian military at the door step of India since 1860. Alarmed by the prospect of complete suspension of her trade with China through Eastern Turkistan by the emergence of this newly independent country, Russian army moved towards Kashgar as if to swallow the place in order to create pressure upon Turkistan so that her trade with China was not impaired.

Both British and Russia attempted vigorously to woo Yakoob Beg and this made the Central Asian country politically important. However, in this race the British won. A trade agreement with Yakoob Beg was concluded in April 1870 by which all transit dues on goods passing between British India and Turkistan were abolished.[27] A regular trade between India and Eastern Turkistan began to flow. Kashmir and Punjab were two important centres of India-Turkistan trade.

A list of import from Eastern Turkistan is given below[28] :

Commodity	Prices in Turkistan	Prices in the Punjab
	Amount in Rs.	Amount in Rs.
Charas per pound	20 to 30	60 to 80
Gold dust per tola	14-0-0	15-8-0
Gold coins	5-0-0	5-0-0
Peshru per maund	40 to 50	100 to 120
Raw silk per maund	160 to 200	240 to 300
Exports from Eastern Turkistan		
	Prices in Turkistan	Prices in the Punjab
Sugar per maund	14-0-0	50-0-0
Honey ,,	8-0-0	40-0-0
Pepper ,,	30 0-0	70-0-0
Ginger ,,	8-0-0	25-0-0
Tea (Green) ,,	80-0-0	150-0-0
Indigo ,,	80-0-0	150-0-0
Opium ,,	280-0-0	415-0-0
Brocade ,,	55 to 100-0-0	100 to 150-0-0
Muslin per *than*	3-0-0	5-0-0

But this trade could not be carried on uninterrupted. The ever increasing British influence did not last long. The Turkistans themselves soon became averse to fostering good relation with British India. As a corollary, Russia-Turkistan relation began to be improved and eventually a treaty was concluded in June 1872 between them[29]. Yakoob had no faith on the Russians. Therefore, in 1874 again a commercial treaty was concluded with the English and it continued until the Chinese army captured this country in 1877[30] and the British in India dared not to interfere.

A.I. Chicherov has referred the efforts to develop Russian trade with India in the 18th century were practically dropped on acoount of political crisis.[31] But this is not correct. Activities and efforts of the Tarist Government to devise ways and means to develop trade were made upto 1801.

REFERENCES

1. Vinacke, *H.M. A History of the Far East in Modern Times.* (London 1960), p. 393.

2. Turner, S. An *Acccount of Embassy to the Court of Teshoo Lama in Tibet* (Land. 1809), P. 374.

3. *Ibid.* All the attempts on the part of Russia, Turner observes, proved to be short-lived because of the watchful jealousy of the Chinese and the disinclination of the Tibetans. But this obervation appears to be an exaggeration.

4. Markham, C.R. *Narratives of the Missiou of G. Bogle to Tibet and of the journey of Thomas Manning to Lhasa* (Lond. 1876) P. 162, Markham notes that the term Kalmukh is the equivalent for the Manchurians. This is wrong.

5. *Ibid*, pp. 125-26
6. *Ibid*.
7. *Ibid*. p. 160
8. *Ibid*.
9. *Ibid*. pp 125-26
10. Sec my article published [in *The Historical Review*', Vol. I, No. 2 (July-December, 1987) for detailed description of Bogle.

11. Panchen Lama was not the ruler of Tibet. The ruler was Dalai Lama and Panchan Lama acted as his deputy.

12. *Home Misc.* Vol. 219, p. 377.

13. *Ibid.*

14. *Ibid.* p. 378

15. About the identity of [Dorjieff or Dorzhievy there are at least three versions :

  (i) He was described as first *Tsaint Hamba* to the Dalai Lama of Tibet. He was sent by the Dalai to St. Petersburg in 1900 with important diplomatic mission. His mission was described as 'Extraordinary Mission' and its object was a 'rapproachment, and the strengthen of good relations with Russia'.

  (ii) He was by [brith a Buriat of Chovinskaia, in Trans Baikalia, Erstern Siberia and was brought up in the province of Azochozki. He had settled himself in Tibet in 1880 (In that case his arrival in Tibet in 1900 is wrong).

  (iii) He was a Mongolian Buriat of Russian origin, who came occasionally to Russia with the object of making money collections for his Order from the numerous Buddhists in the Russian Empire. His visit to Russia had no official character whatever, although he was accompanied on this visit by other Tibetans. For further [discussion consult Sir Francis Younghuband's *India and Tibet,* pp. 66-70.

Anolher reference to Dorjieff is known from Kawaguchi, the courageous Japanese traveller himself a Buddhist, and once Recter of a monastery in Japan, who lived in the Sera Monastory. His valuable work, *Three years in Tibet* in which he has given details of Dorjieff's pamphlet.

16. Young husband *op. cit.*, p. 393

17. *Ibid.*

18. Vinacke, *Op. cit.*, p, 311

19. Hodgson, B.H. *Essays on Languages Literature and Religion of Nepal and Tibet together with further papers in the geography, Ethnology and [Commerce of those countries* (Lond. 1874). Pt. II, Sec. VIII, pp. 95-96.

20. *Ibid,*

21. Markham, *Op. cit.*, p. 137

22. *Ibid.*

23. For further discussion [See Prof. J.N. Sarkar's *Thoughts on the study of Indian History,* an address delivered ty him as a General President of I. H.C. XXVII held at Calicut University, December 1976.

24. *Ibid.*

25. *Ibid.*

26. *Home Department Consultations,* 22 Dec. 1793. An Indian merchant Sheikh Bhilk by name, has been mentioned in the record of 1577, who carried on trading activities with Russia. It records that 'in 1577 one Sheikh Bhik, who used to trade in Maldahi Cloths, (Cloths of Malda, a district town of North Bengal, India) set sail for Russia with three ships laden with silk cloths, and that two of the ships were wrecked somewhere in the neighbourhood of the Persian Gulf'vide *Bengal District Cazetteers,* Malda, by G.E. Lambourn (Calcutta, 1918) p. 59.

From the above description of Sheikh Bhik (? Bhiku) it appears that Indo-Russian sea bourne trade was of long standing and was carried on through Persian Gulf. Indian ships got unloaded at Bandar Abbas or Bushire, one of the two important ports, on the Persian Gulf. From here one ove rland route went to the Caspian Sea for Astrakhan, while the other went West to Bukhara.

27. *Foreign Deptt. Records, Pol. (A) Cons.* 216, June 1870, Vicerory to Yakoob Beg.

28. Figures are taken from the article of B.G. Gill. *Trade and Diplomacy in Eastern Turkistan, 1864-78,* pp 290-91 Published in the Journal, India, Past and Present Vol, 3, No 2 (Bombay, 1986).

29. Aitchison, C.U. (ed) op. cit., Vol XIV, p. 2.

30. Boulger,, D.C. *Life of Yakoob Beg* (Lond.) 1878), p. 118.

31. Chicherov, A.l. *India : Economic Development in 16th to 18th Centuries* (Moscow, 1971) p. 109.

EPILOGUE

I

Now we would like to investigate some interesting points to reveal British Home Government's policy in regard to Tibet. Not many would dispute the importance of isolating Home Government's views which we have seen emboldened China to try to establish her sphere of influence in Tibet. The fact is, however, that little headway has so far been made in this direction and in the case study I offer the argument is much too general to be useful in such contexts. The reason is that the disposal of the investigation do not normally lend us to this kind of an enquiry. Wnen discussing in the light of contemporary diplomatic manoeuvres, our understanding in this case should be judged by the political and economic interests of the British Home Government in this region.

No doubt, the Chinese in the twentieth century, undertook a grave risk by imposing her territorial overlordship on Tibat completely ignoring world opinion. Her role as saviour of people's liberty appears to be a big hoax.

But why she did it ? What was her motive behind it ? To know this once again we should turn our attention to the strategical position of Tibet. Based on Tibet any country militarily powerful can design to disorganize India's internal economy and destroy its morale. Settling herself on India's shoulder, no doubt, China has been successful in her attempt to compel India to spend bulk of its wealth for maintaining large army to defend her border with Tibet and thus draining wealth from her fund reserved for agricultural and industrial develop.-ment.

Long before, the field was prepared by the Home Government of Britain which enabled China to use Tibet as happy-hunting ground. Now let us see how did it take place.

Obstructed by the Tibetans, the Indian merchants and the Europeans, especially the English stopped visiting, Tibet, though the Tibetans were allowed to come to India without any hindrance whenever and wherever they liked. Taking stock of the entire situation, the Government of India in 1873 decided to write to the Peking authorities requesting "for an order of admittance to Tibet and the authorities at Peking should allow a renewal of the friendly intercourse between India and Tibet which existed in the days of Bogle and Turner". It is really difficult to understand the reason of writing to the Peking authorities for permission for entry into Tibet though the British government in India had easy access to Tibetan hierarchy and was fully aware of Tibeto—Chinese bitter relations. Be that as it may, the British recognised Chinese overlordship on Tibet not without reason.

This recognition, no doubt emboldened the Peking authorities to create several complications in future aggrevating Sino-Indian relations to worse. Heinrich Harrer[1], a German national and eye witness to the events in Tibet on the eve of Chinese occupation hold in his book "*Seven Years in Tibet*":

"The threatening attitude of China, though traditional has now again been intensified. Every Chinese government, whether imperial, national or Communist, had always professed to regard Tibet as a Chinese province. This pretension was entirely contrary to the wishes of the Tibetans, who loved their independence and were clearly entitled to enjoy it".

Mr. Blanford shared the same impression long before Heinrich Harrer. In 1870 when he reached near India—Tibet border, the Commandant of Khampa Jong met him and assured him that the Tibetans had no ill-will to foreigners and not at all reluctant to receive the Europeans. Bu tit was the-

Chinese who were playing dirty tricks in Tibet and forcing the Tibetan hierarchy to keep shut the door of Tibet to the foreigners. But if the foreigners wished to negotiate directly with the Tibetan authorities for obtaining entry-permit for entering into Tibet, they could do it. Although the Chinese had stationed their troops in Tibet, the British in India had nothing to fear,[2] he held.

It appears that the Chinese had stationed a garrison in Tibet to intimidate them. Surprisingly this Chinese unethical measure was supported by the Lieutenant Governor of Bengal.

"He fully sympathised with the Chinese desire..."

Familiarity gained by practical experience and knowledge on the Himalayan states and their internal state of politics, people like Sir Francis Younghusband expressed deep concern for British policy to allow China a free hand in Tibet despite her bitter antagonism against China and which was no secret at all to the British authorities in India. It was also known to them that China had very "little real control over the local government" of Tibet.[3] Younghusband therefore, assumed that the policy pursued by the Home Government was not "necessarily the best". It was by no means unlikely that China would be able to seize the opportunity to wipe out Tibetan resistance.

Apprehended by the Chinese high handedness in Tibet, the latter cherished the idea of keeping close contact with British India. Proof of which can be obtained, from Mr. Blanford's evidence given earlier. It can be assumed that the government of India duly informed the status of Tibet and its situation to the Home Government. The latter, on the other hand, issued specific instruction not to open direct negotiation with Tibet but *via* China.

As a corollary, Tibet avowedly opposed all such British attempts of sending its mission to Tibet and her opposition to China continued as before. At this stage, Tibet had to face two enemies—China and the British. In 1890 Chefu convention was concluded between Britain and China and under which the latter undertook to protect "any mission which should be sent to Tibet" by the British authorities in India. But when actually a mission was sent to Tibet the undertaking proved literally valueless, for "they (the Chinese) were unable to afford it the slightest protection". The Chinese representative in Lhasa confessed that he was not even allowed by the Tibetans to meet the British mission.[4]

One thingh we should keep in view in this connection that the Tibetan authorities were not wholly reluctant to keep the foreigners out of Tibet. But the two foreign countries China and Britain made the situation worse for them. On the one hand, China wanted to keep Tibet within her own influence, on the other, she allowed British mission to enter into that country despite knowing fully well that right to admission in Tibet depended still that time wholly on Tibetan authorities and not on the Chinese and therefore, the British were not allowed to enter. Naturally the convention of 1890 proved useless, and the outcome might have had anticipated by the Chinese.

And again, repeated appeal of the Tibetan hierarchy to the British government in India, when her national security was at stake by Nepal's aggression and Chinese insistence to keep her army in Tibet, failed to receive any positive response, made her position helpless. Militarily week she failed to accomplish anything in matters of foreign trade or diplomatic relations with other countries in the face of stiff resistance by the Chinese. The activities of Britain has been aptly observed below :

"The British, playing politics with the Chinese at the time, at first chose to support China's claim to authority over Tibet and signed various treaties with China concerning Tibet. This made the Tibetans aware of the danger of their position...".

The conclusion of Treaty with the Chinese, evidently endangered the safety and security of Tibet. This ensures us that China had probably enjoyed the authority of inflicting damage to Tibet's independence. But the actual position of China can be grasped from the following extracts :

"....... upto that point they (Tibetans) had only had China

to contend with and had always managed to keep her at a comfortable arm's length ; the existence of the two Chinese Ambans at Lhasa was an effective face—shaven for China and the Tibetans saw no harm in allowing her to pretend to an authority that she could not enforce in fact."

At this stage a dispute arose between England and China over England's attempt to export Indian tea to Tibet. Indian tea began growing in large quantities and found a prospective market in Tibet. But "an absolute embargo is laid on anything the shape of Tea". Besides tea, Manchester and Birmingham goods and Indian indigo would find a market in Tibet, and in return Tibetan wool, sheep, cattle, walnuts, Tibetan cloths and other commodities could have been imported to India. The Peking authorities had in no way encouraged the British to sell tea in Tibet.[5]

".........the Chinese in spite of concessions in other matters by the Government of India, remained obstinate and still remain obstinate, in regard to the admission of tea. and eventually only agreed to admit Indian tea into Tibet at a rate of duty not exceeding that at which Chinese tea is imported into England, which, as the latter rate of duty is 6d. per pound..."[6]

At this stage, the Home government in England opened negotiation with the Peking authorities for mutual co-operation in the field of commerce and the British government also requested them to exert pressure on the Tibetan authorities so that the latter come to terms in matters of commerce with the British in India, which they could easily do by direct negotiation with Tibet.

On December 5, 1893 the Trade Regulations were signed at Darjeeling between the British Political officer in Sikkim and the Chinese frontier officer, a representative of Chinese Resident at Lhasa. Accordingly, a trade mart at Yatung was to "be open for all British subjects for purposes of trade" from 1st May, 1894. But what was the out come of this effort ? The Tibetan authorities refused to accept the clauses of the treaty. Naturally the treaty appeared to be useless. No fruitful result was obtained by the British and the Chinese could

not be able to compel the Lhasa authorities to accept the terms
of the treaty. This appears that China had no real control on
Tibet at this stage and the latter tried utmost to remain as an
independent state disowning China's watchful control on her.
So what we find is that the Lhasa authorities were obviously
reluctant to accept any uncalled for Chinese overture arising
out of agreement concluded between China and other country.
China undoubtedly tried to compel Tibet to accept the
terms of the agreement but it lay in tatters. The British
government in India found that the Chinese though friendly to
them "had no authority whatever".   China confessed that the
Tibetans were unmanagable and they would not obey the
Chinese[7].

"It has always been recognised", the despatch of Government of India continues, "that the utmost patient is necessary
in dealing with the Tibetans and having regard to the short
time which has elapsed since the date fixed for the opening of
the Yatung mart, the Governor General-in-Council would
prefer to make nothing in the nature of a complaint to the
Chinese Government at the present stage".[8]

While Bengal government was impatient to settle the matter
with the Tibetan officials at Lhasa, the British authorities in
London were persistently inclined to open a negotiation between London and Peking. Bengal Government was asked to
"take a wider view, and display a calmer spirit, and greater
confidence in the wisdom and sagacity of their London
rulers"[9]. It clearly appears that the Bengal Government was
in dark in matters of Home government's Tibet-Policy and
neither the latter disclose its mind to the Bengal government
nor the latter was granted freedom to open negotiation with
Tibet directly. Some times later when the Bengal Government
made a reasonable request to open talk with the Lhasa authorities,"..............the House of Commons, which controls the
destinies of the empire, was still asking why we did not apply
to the Chinese, the local Officers' faith in the superior efficacy
of headquarters' treatment is somewhat shaken[10].

Undoubtedly, the Bengal Government was better informed
about the internal position of Tibet than the London authorities. But the latter deliberately trying to give much impor-

tance to the Peking authorities in matters of Tibetan affairs and the Bengal Government did not concede its surprise. It put up question with profound amazement :

".........expect so much from the Chinese Central Government which has so, little real control over the local Governments."

But the London authorities did not stop carrying correspondence with the Chinese government. Sir Francis Young husband lamented :

"Whether matter which, after forming the subject to voluminous correspondence between the provincial Government and the Government of India, between the latter and the India office, between the India Office and the Foreign Office, between the Foreign Office and the Ambassador abroad, between him and the Foreign Government, which are discussed in the Cabinet and form a subject for debate in the House of Commons and the House of Lords, and for platform speeches and newspapers articles innumerable, do not in this lengthy process assume a magnitude which they never originally possessed ; whether having assumed such magnitude, they ever really do get settled or only compromised ; and whether after all, they might not have been settled expeditiously and decisively on the spot before they had been allowed to grow to these alarming positions"[12].

Dispassionate testimony of this English observer concludes :

"At any rate it cannot be safely assumed that the Central Governmet method is necessarily the best. In this case, for instance, all that resulted was that the Chinese Government in the Chefu Convention concluded three years later, undertook to protect any mission which should be sent to Tibet an understanding which was literally valueless for when a mission was actually sent to Tibet they were unable to afford it the slightest protection..."[13]

However, no improvement in relation with Tibet was possible only because of lapses on the part of the Bengal Government to hold talks directly with the Tibetan hierarchy to normalise the relation except;

" ....improving the road inside our (British India) frontier, and with doing what they could on our side to entice and further trade".[14]

Colman Macaulay, Secretary of the Bengal Government, reviewed the entire situation and decided to come to terms with Tibet. He himself visited the frontier and reached near Shigatse in 1885 by the route up the head of the Sikkim Valley, when he saw a local Tibetan official coming from the other side. He began discussing with the Tibetan Official and then he came to know that the Tibetan administration keenly desired to enter into "friendly relationship" with British India. Maculay threw his whole energy to develop the relation. On his insistence the Secretary of State for India organised a mission under the leadership of Macaulay. But to Macaulay's astonishment, the mission was directed to send to China, though on the eve of starting from Darjeeling to Tibet when "international considerations" came in and Government revoked the proposal.[15]

At this stage Tibet launched an unprovoked aggression on feudatory state of British India. The attack was repulsed by the British army. Eventually, in 1890 a settlement was effected.[16] The attack reveals a number of consequences :

Firstly, British authorities in India solicited Chinese help to procure withdrawal of the Tibetans. But ignoring Chinese insistence the Tibetans continued their onslaught. Therefore, Chinese protests lay in tatters. At the same time, it cleared the position of the Chinese in Tibet who had no control on that country.

Secondly, although China had no say in matters of Tibet, the British authorities signed a convention with the Chinese Resident in Calcutta, on March 17, 1890 allowing them to take part in the discussion of Indo-Tibet boundary. By the convention both the British and Chinese government agreed :

" ....reciprocally to respect the boundary as defined in

Article one and to prevent acts of aggression from their respective sides of the frontier"[17] (though there was less possibility of Chinese aggression during that time).

As a result of inclusion of the Chinese in the convention, the Tibetans never recognised the Convention.

Finally, it is worthwhile to mention here that the British Government in London deliberately brought or included China in the discussion on Anglo-Tibet relation. What motive lay behind this British plan ? We have discussed this plan in the subsequent chapter with other problems. Here we have singled out the British plan.

The Home Government in England neither wanted to conquer Tibet and include it as one of the states of India, nor wanted to impose any political control on Tibet. On the contrary, the British authorities did not want to keep Tibet vaccum and, therefore, supported China whole heartedly to impose her political authority on Tibet. Obviously, this exacerbated Sino-Tibet as well as India—Tibet relations. With India, Nepal, Sikkim, Bhutan and Burma all under British influence, and with the British evidently supporting the Chinese demand over Tibet, the position took completely different turn.

At this stage, the thirteenth Gyalwa Rimpoche "sent an envoy to the Tsar of Russia to open negotiations. The Tsar was much interested, not only with an eye to trade, but also with the thought of using Tibet as a convenient back door in China".

Now the realisation dawned on the British by Tibet's attempt to conclude secret treaty with Russia, that China totally failed to improve her image in Tibet, nay Tibet completely established herself as an independent country.

"Realizing that in effect Tibet was not the vassal of China that she supposed, Britain promptly repudiated her previous recognition of Chinese 'authority' and sent an armed expedition, under sir Francis Young husband, into Tibet".

From the above extract it is found, Britain was not aware

of China's real position in Tibet. It is an archaic lie. She knew every thing but she did not repudiate China's demand on Tibet so long her interests were at stake.

Challenged by British arms Gyalwa Rimpoche fled to Peking "to enter negotiations with the Empress". By this time "the British signed a Treaty with the Tibetan Government and withdrew their force, leaving behind only a small commission." Britain attempted to pursuade Russia to recognize that Tibet was "independent of China and Tibet should remain closed to all foreign penetration" Gyalwa Rimpoche then came to India with the request to help him drawing the Chinese out of Tibet. At this stage 'internal revolt' placed China in a difficult situation and "The Tibetan who had been keeping the Chinese at bay now had no difficulty in drawing them out".

China's futile attempt to depose Rimpoche was encountered by him by deporting "all Chinese residents in Tibet" and "issued a Declaration of Independence" deporting the "Ambans" out of the country[18].

EPILOGUE

II

Finally let us analyse the whole situation in an interrogative manner.

The foregoing analytical study of Trans-Himalayan trade A Politico: Economic relations of India, Tibet and China for the period of 1774-1914 shows different currents and cross-currents shaping British India's Himalayan Frontier policy. It seeks to throw light on some aspects of India's border issue with Tibet and China and the latter's controversial demand on Tibet as her vassal state.

The matter is so complicated that it has been difficult to define the political status of Tibet. Tibet was not absolutely independent, during the period of our discussion, in the fullest sense of the term, but in most respects we have treated her as an independent state, having power to declare war and treaties. She was normally tributary to China Government evidently regarded her as lying outside the limits of the Chinese Empire.

The turbulent population of Tibet became mild and meek after being baptised in Buddhism. They maintained no regular army. Because they did not anticipate any invasion neither from north nor from south. The case of switzerland may be referred to in this connection. The imperialist China overawed them and repeatedly attempted to impose her political hegemony over Tibet. At least on two occasions, we have seen, the Tibetans overthrew Chinese authority, drove their political agents away from Lhasa and massacred Chinese troops. But fresh importation of troops from Chinese mainland rode roughshod over Tibet and put down the revolt with a vengeance.[19]

Now let us turn our attention to the question—how was Tibet treated by the Chinese Government ? Wnat was its status ? Was there any treaty or agreement between two countries ? Obviously answer to these questions are confusing.

The confusion over Tibet's political identity since the begining of the present century should be attributed solely to British machinations. By its own admission China at no time exercised real authority over Tibet.

But the English East India Company favoured the idea of Chinese hold on Tibet. Therefore, it is not true that during its formative years, the East India Company desired to keep an independent Tibet as a buffer state, between India and Russia on one hand and between India and China on the other. In fact, it seems that the British Government in India blatantly encouraged the Peking authorities to keep Tibet as her protectorate denying the right and freedom of the Tibetans to rule their country by themselves only to keep Russia away. In the preceding chapter we have seen Russia was trying to enter into Tibet. The object was perhaps to find an entry to Persian Gulf.

The reason behind this British policy is not very difficult to find out. Reviewing contemporary political situation of this part of Asia, it appears that the British authorities in India preferred China to Russia holding some political influence on the Tibetan authorities in Lhasa, because the former was too weak to pose any threat to India, a British colony. And again, it would not be possible for the Chinese to remain powerful in Tibet in the face of relentless Tibetan struggle against them. It would serve two purposes at the same time.

Firstly, the Peking authorities, in response to the British support to their Tibetan policy the English East India Company thought, would not be unkind to their entry into the markets of China through Tibet.

Secondly, Peking's presence in Tibet would not allow Russia to infiltrate into that country.

Allowing Chinese free hand in Tibet, the British eventually found the Chinese prohibition was the sole obstacle to British commercial interests in Tibet. So they thought to take up the matter with the Peking authorities.[20] But the negotiation bore no fruit.

Opposed by the Tibetan resistance, the Peking authorities could not effectively impose their political authority on Tibet and also prevented the English Company from entering into Chinese market.

So the company authorities in India changed their policy in respect to Tibet and wanted to see Tibet an independent state. They acknowledged Tibet's right to conclude treaties at the end of the Younghusband expedition in 1904 and the Simla convention of 1913-14. Tibet also declined to allow China to take part in the negotiation with the Younghusband mission. Dalai Lama did not provide transport to the Chinese *Amban* to meet the mission.[21]

Sir Frederick O' Connor, who went with the expedition as its Political Secretary held that the facts clearly indicated the inability of the Chinese to make good their claim to exercise control over the Tibetans, in any respect, whether as regards their internal or external policy.[22]

Tibetans were a different stock of people from the Chinese. They have no similarity with the Chinese except in religion of pre-revolutionary China, and even in religious practice, there was an impassable difference. The introduction and spread of Buddhism in Tibet constitute a considerable part of Tibet's historical relation with India. Since the Seventh Century (A.D) when Sron-Btsan-Sgam. Po (B. 617 A.D) became the ruler of Tibet, there has been a great spiritual and cultural exchange between India and Tibet. Large number of Indian theologists and Buddhist monks came to Tibet at the invitation of her kings. Tibetan language which till then had no alphabate found its asylum in Indian epigraphy, phonetics and grammer. Chinese pictorial alphabate spreaded to Japan and Korea whereas Tibet did not accept it. On the contrary, she turned her attention towards India and accepted traditional *Nagri* script. It indicates Tibet's preference. She could not stand China, disliked her arrogance and attempt to subdue her. Thonmi-Sambho-ta who is said to be the father of Tibetan literature came to India, studied Indian phonetics and grammer in the Nalanda University and eventually invented alphabetical script for Tibetan language.

The political status of Tibet and Nepal was almost similar. Both were nominally tributary to China. China's nominal suzerainty over Nepal got recognition for the first time after the Tibeto-Nepal war (1788-92) and reiterated in the treaty of 1856 did not, however, lead to strengthen her position in Nepal.[23] The only difference between Tibet and Nepal was that, while China actively interferred in the internal affairs of the former through her *Ambans* posted in Lhasa, she remained satisfied with the annual tribute paid by the latter.

Uptil 1792 Tibet remained as Chinese protectorate. Thereafter China left Tibet free to organize her own defence. When Zorawar Singh, the Dogra General, launched an attack on Tibet in 1841, China did not come to rescue her.

Nepal attacked Tibet again in 1856, exacted from her free trade concessions, an annual payment of Rs. 10,000 and even extra-territorial rights.[24] But no Chinese help came and again when British army marched upon the Capital of Sikkim the ruler of the country accepted British terms in 1861. China remained silent though Sikkim had political, commercial and ecclesiastical relations and whose princes were closely connected with Tibet by matrimonial relations and therefore, China had a moral obligation to Sikkim because of her close relation (as she demanded) with Tibet. On the contrary, Sikkim helped the British in the Gurkha war of 1814 ignoring the Chinese *Amban* in Tibet who had written a number of letters to the Sikkim Durbar desiring to place troops at Gyantse and Phari for the :

"convenience of making enquiries into the movement of Feringis (English) and that the Sikkim *Durbar* need not entertain any fear on that score..."[25]

British expedition under Sir Francis Younghusband was led into Tibet in 1904. China did not come to rescue her and this time Tibet did not seek help from China. This is because Tibet loved to maintain independent status in international position and her past experience (in 1791) about Chinese conduct was not at all satisfactory.

Tibet declined to comply with the decision taken at the Anglo-Chinese convention of 1890, regarding Tibet's boundary with Sikkim. Another settlement became necessary between Britain and Tibet in 1904 for the latter's acceptance of the decision taken at the earlier Convention with China. In all the boundary disputes and settlements between Tibet and her neighbouring states, the former had been a signatory on its own right. These agreements included treaty between Tibet and Ladakh in 1684, treaty between China and Tibet in 1842, treaty between Tibet and Nepal in 1856 and also in the Convention of 1914 between Great Britain on the one side and Tibet and China on the other.

It has already been mentioned that Tibet was afraid of British imperialism and therefore, sought the presence of China despite her malignity only to counter British penetration. The diplomacy pursued by her proved to be a foolish measure in near future. To avoid

British infiltration she accepted Chinese control over her who appeared to be a vicious enemy. Similar diplomacy undertook by Bhutan when the former sought Chinese assistance in 1864 against British threat. China, however, declined to get involved in British action against Bhutan.

In Tibet, there was again rivalry between the authorities of Lhasa and Shigatse weakening greatly their capacity of concerted counter measures against their common foe, the Chinese.

China regarded Tibet a 'barbarous' country, just very near to her border, has no right to live independently. This is an universal imperial consensus. China's such stand was largely due to British chicanery in the name of diplomacy when British did not defy, in the preposterous Anglo-Russian Convention of 1907, China's suzerainty over Tibet.

As regards to trade and commerce, Tibet had close contact with Nepal, Bhutan, India and China too. Occasionally, the Kalmukhs, the Russian merchants, came to Tibet to sell their commodities and buy Indian goods. Indian merchants were specially treated by the Tibetans and Indian commodities were in greater demand there especially to Chinese buyers. Indian merchants found no restriction. Trouble ensued when the English began consolidating their political power in India, the tiny states of the Himalayas were suspicious.

With the expansion of British rule towards north-east of India, Tibet began to feel pulsating pressure. China, in response, sought to strengthen her control in Tibet which promoted her insatiable desire to keep Tibet prostrate at her feet. She repeatedly propagated that Tibet was an inalianable part of the Chinese territory intending to keep British imperialism away from Tibet.

Torned by Opium war (1834-42) and T'ai P'ing rebellion (1851-1864) imperial China failed to rise to the occasion when British power invaded Tibet in 1904. In total disregard of the basic norms governing international relationship, the Chinese went so far as to openely provide a forum for the Chinese representatives' political activities of preaching Tibet had never been an independent country undermining the unity and independence of Tibet. The Lamas, especially the Dalai Lamas, many a times expressed indignition at such an act of interferring in Tibet's internal affairs and harming Indo-Tibet religio-cultural-commercial relations.

The above discussions make it clear that the Tibeto-China relations was essentially a querulous, trading charges, holding one another responsible for the carnage often done by both sides posing threats of serious breach of peace in the Himalyan region.

The whole attitude of China towards Tibet took a drastic change after the Chinese revolution. The entire political situation of this area proceeded to change. She held that it was her responsibility to modernise Tibet by forcing her ideology to impose and thus compel Tibet's markets open to Chinese industry and for fresh source of raw materials. Tibet's markets were extremely limited and the purchasing capacity of the vast majority of the people was extremely negligible, though the possibility of getting raw materials was enormous.

So long British power remained in India, they demonstrated that they had the power to intervene in Tibet whenever they liked and neither the Chinese nor the Dalai Lama could stop them from doing so.

The people Republic of China only after the departure of the British from this region became active in South Asia and swallowed Tibet. Chau-en-Lai's attempt in the 1950s to establish friendly relation with Asian countries was only an eyewash for his future invasion of Tibet.

Being not get flustered by the persistent Chinese elusiveness the British were unable to clinch the repeated attempts they made to settle the boundary. To-day's conditions are totally different. The gaps between India and China have been widened. The mutual distrust, staying in opposite camps have made the situation worse. Nevertheless, war will not bring about final settlement and the difficulties are not insuperable. But at the same time we should remember that the Chinese are not such stock of people to be easily pursuaded or yielded, on the contrary, they are dangerous if and when they find softness or weakness in the opponent.

REFERENCES

1. Heinrich Harrer was a prisoner of war in India during the Second World War. Ecaped from the Internment Camp, he fled into Tibet and lived there until he was forced to leave on the eve of the Chinese occupation in 1949. R.K. Chatterjee, *India's Land Borders*, p. 81

2. *Blue Book*, p. 24

3. Young husband, Sir Francis—*India and Tibet*, p. 45

4. *Ibid.* p. 46

5. Thugten J. Norbu & Collin Turnbull, *Tibet*, p. 317.
   (Penguin Book), Lond. 1969

6. *Blue Book*, p. 52

7. *Ibid.* p. 24

8. *Ibid*, p. 31

9. Young husband, *Op. Cit.*, p. 45

10. *Ibid.*

11. *Ibid.*

12. *Ibid.*

13. *Ibid.* pp. 45-46

14. *Ibid.* p. 46

15. *Ibid.* pp. 46-47

16. *Blue Book*, p. 24

17. *Ibid.* p. 31

18. Norbu & Turnbull. *op. cit.* pp. 317-18

19. Majumder, British attitude to Nepal's Relation with Tibet and China, *Bengal Past and Present* (Diamond Jubilee). 1967, p. 167.

20. BLG (*p*) *Pr.* September (1870)

21. Richardson, *Tibet and its Htstory* (Lond. 1962)

22. Young husband, *op. cit.* p. 49

23. Majumder, *op. cit,*

24. P.K. Jha, *History of Sikkim*, p. 43.

25. *Ibid.*, p. 107

SELECT SOURCES AND BIBLIOGRAPHY[1] ORIGINAL SOURCES (UNPUBLISHED) INDIA OFFICE LIBRARY LONDON

Bengal Public Consultations, 1790
Bogle Papers MSS. E/226
Foreign Department, Records, Pol. (A) Cons. 216, June, 1870
Governor General's Proceedings, 1779.
Home Department Consultations, 1771
Home miscellaneous, Vol. 219, Vol. 608
India Office Records, Correspondence Reports White Paper, I.

Government Sources
(Published)

Bengal Lt. Governor's Proceedings (Pol.) 1859-1892

	Report on the External trade of Bengal with Nepal, Sikkim, Bhutan, Tibet (1880-1903).
Edgar, J.W	Report on a visit to Sikkim and Tibetan Frontier in October, November, December, 1873 Calcutta, 1879.
Macaulay, C.	Report on a Mission to Sikkim and Tibetan frontier, Calcutta, 1885.

Books (English)

Aitchison, C.U.	A collection of Treatise, Engagements and Sanads relating to India and Neighbouring countries, Calcutta, 1863.

---

1. The list of books mentioned only the works that have a more or less direct bearing on the topics. It does not include a number of other books and articles cited in the notes to support minor points and digression.

Auber, P.	China, an outline of its Government, Laws and Policy, Lond. 1834.
Balkrishna	Commercial Relations between India and England.
Bart, Staunton	An Authentic Account of Embassy from Great Britain to the Emperer of China, Vol. 2, Lond. 1797.
Barrow, J.	Some Account of the public life and a Selection of the unpublished writings of the Earl of Macartney, Vol. 2, Lond. 1807.
Bell, Charles	Tibet Past and present, Oxford 1924. Portrait of the Dalai Lama, Lond. 1946.
Boulger, D.C.	Life of Yakoob beg, Lond, 1878.
Buchanan, Francis.	An Account of District of Purnea in 1809.
Cammann, S	The Panchen Lama's visit to China in 1780.
Chapman, F. Spencer	Lhasa, the Holy City, Lond. 1938
Chakrabarti, P.N.	Anglo—Mughal Commercial Relations, 1583-1717. (cal. 1983)
Chaudhuri, K.C.	Anglo-Nepalese Relations, Calcutta, 1950.
Chicherov, A.I.	India : Economic Development in 16th to 18th centuries, Moscow, 1971.
Cipolla, C.M.	The Fontana Economic History of Europe, Vol. 2.
Das, Taraknath[2]	British expansion in Tibet, Calcutta, 1922
Davies, A.M.	Warren Hastings, Lond. 1936.

---

2. The author has been described by the British Writers as fanatically anti--British.

Desideri, I.	An account of Tibet (ed. F. de Filippi) Lond. 1932, introduction by C.J. Wessels (revised edition). A valuable England's pioneer to India and Burma, His Companies and contemporaries with his Narrative told in his wards (ed. Hak. Soc.), Lond. 1698.
Fitzerald, C.P.	China, A Short Cultural History, New York and Lond. 1938.
Foster, W.	The English Factories in India, 1942-45.
Francke, A.H.	The kingdom of GNYA-KHARI-St Sampo, the first king of Tibet.
Graham Sandberg :	The Exploration of Tibet, its history and particulars, Lond. 1911, P. 164
Hakluyt, Richard	The principal Navigations etc. Vol. II Lond. 1579.
Hodgson, B.H.	Essays of Languages, Literature and Religion of Nepal and Tibet together with further papers pt. 11, Lond. 1974.
Hunter, W.W.	The life of B.H. Hodgson.
Kawaguchi, E.	Three years in Tibet, Benaras 1909.
Kirk Partick, Col.	An Account of the Kindom of Nepal, Lond. 1811.
Lamb, A.	Britain and Chinese Central Asia, The Road to Lhasa, 1765-1905, Lond. 1960.
Lattimore, Owen.	Inner Asian Frontiers of China, New york 1940.
Laufer, B	Was Odoric of Pordenone ever in Tibet.
Li, T.T.	Historical status of Tibet. New York, 1956.
Markham, C.R.(cd).	Narratives of the Mission of George Bogle to Tibet and of Journey of Thomas Manning of Lhasa, Lond. 1876.

Morse, H.B.   The Chronicles of the East India Company's trading to China, Vol. 2, oxford, 1926

Norbu, Thubten Jigme Tibet, Middlesex, U.K. 1969.
    &
Colin Turnbull

Petech, L.   The Mission of Bogle and Turner according to Tibetan Text, Leyden, 1950.

Regmi, D.R.   Medieval Nepal, Pt. I. Cal. 1965.

Richardson   Tibet and its History, Lond. 1962.

Rockhill, W.W.   Life of Buddha, Lond. 1844.
    Do   The Dalai Lamas and their Relations with the Manchu Emperors of China.

Sandberg, Graham.   The Exploration of Tibet, Cal. & Lond., 1904.

Sanwal, B.D.   Nepal and the East India Company, Bombay, '65.

Sarkar, J.N.   The Life of Mirjumla (2nd. ed.)
    Do   Thoughts on the study of Indian History

Satstri, G.C.   Historical Glimpses of Modern Nepal, Kathmandu,

Sen, Jahar   Indo-Nepal Trade in the 19th Century, Cal. 1977.

Thomson, J.C.   History of Ancient Geography, Cambridge, '48.

Turner, S.   An Account of an Embassy to the Court of Teshu Lama in Tibet, Lond. 1809.

Vinacke, Harold M.   A History of the Far East in Modern Times, Lond. 1960.

Wadell, L.A.   The Buddhism of Tibet of Lamaism (2nd ed.), Cambridge, 1939.

Wessells, C. (S.J.)   Early Jesuit Travellers in Central Asia 1603-1712, The Hague.

Younghusband, SirF. India and Tibet, Delhi, 1917

Yule, Col.   Marcopolo, Vol. I

JOURNALS, GAZETTERS AND DICTIONERIES

Bengal District Gazetteer, Cal. 1918.

Lambourn, G.E   Malda.
Bengal Past and Present (Diamond Jubilee, 1967).

Majumder   British attitude to Nepal's relation with
                    Tibet and China.
India Past and Present, Vol. 5, No. 2
                        Bombay, 1986.

Gill, B.G.   Trade and Diplomacy in Eastern Turkis-
                    tan, 1864.

The Historical Review Vol. 1 No. 2, 1987

Chakrabarti, P.N.   A Survey of India-Tibetan Trade and
                    Commerce.

J A S B, Vol VIII, No. 3, 1966.

Kachikian, Levon   The Ledger of the Merchant Hovannes
                    Joughayetsi
        J B O R S, Vol. 19, 1903

Diskalkar, D.B.   Macartney Papers
        J R A S, Vol. XII, Lond. 1888

Bushell, S.W.   The Early History of Tibet from Chinese
                    Sources.

J P A S B, Cal. 1910

Francke, Rev. A.H. The kingdom of GNYA-Khribstsampo,
                    the first King of Tibet.
        PIHRC, Vol XIII, 1930.

Sarkar, S.C.   Some notes on the intercourse of Bengal.

Younghusband, Sir F., India and Tibet, Delhi, 1917

Yule, Col.   Marcopolo, Vol. I

JOURNALS, GAZETTEERS AND DICTIONERIES

Bengal District Gazetteer, Cal. 1918.

Lamborn, G.E.   Maldah.

Bengal Past and Present (Diamond Jubilee, 1967).

Majumder   British attitude to Nepal's relation with
Tibet and China.
India Past and Present, Vol. 5, No. 2
Bombay, 1986.

Gill, B.G.   Trade and Diplomacy in Eastern Turkistan, 1804.

The Historical Review Vol. I No. 2, 1987

Chakrabarti, P.N.   A Survey of India-Tibetan Trade and
Commerce.
J.A.S.B. Vol. VIII, No. 2, 1966.

Kaulitian, Jovon   The Ledger of the Merchant Hovhannes
Joughayotsi
J.B.O.R.S., Vol. 19, 1903.

Diskalkar, D.B.   Manuscript Papers
J.R.A.S., Vol. XII, Lond. 1858

Bushell, S.W.   The Early History of Tibet from Chinese
Sources.
J.P.A.S.B. Cal. 1910

Francke, Rev. A.H.   The Kingdom of GNYA-Khribsasampo,
the first King of Tibet.
J.BHRG, Vol XIII, 1910.

Sarkar, S.C.   Some notes off the intercourse of Bengal.

INDEX

A

Abdul Qadir, mission to Tibet, 17, 45

Agreement, of 1779, 48

Altan Khan, 8

Ambans, 10, at Lhasa, 66, 116, 117

Andrade, Antonio, 14

Anglo-Bhutan Treaty, 34

Anglo-Nepal Relations, 65

Anglo-Russian Convention, (1907), 119

Anglo-Tibet Commercial Relations, 90

Anglo-Tibet Diplomatic Relations, 90, 113

Assam, 34 ; strategic Position of, 62

Astrakhan, 97, Indian merchants in, 98

Atish Dipankar Srijnana, 7

B

Bengal, Tibetan traders in, 4 ; unaware of happenings, 16 ;
    trade with Tibet, 22 ; route to Tibet, 22 ; govern-
    ment of, 28, 35, drainage of wealth from, 48 ; trial
    of trade with, Tibet, 50 ; merchants invited to trade
    with Tibet, 51

Bengal Government, Tussle with Home govt. over Tibet, 110 ;
                    relation with Tibet, 111, sought China's
                    help, 112

Bhirukuti, Princess of Nepal, 6, 7

Bhutan, role in trade between Bengal and Tibet, 22 ; overran
        Coochbehar, 32, 34, 44 ; border dispute of 48, 53

Blanford, 106

C

D

H

I

J

K

K'ang- hi, 82
K'ang-Hsi, 73
Kalmukhs, 91, 119
Kashmiri, traders, 20-23
Kashyap Matunga, 13
Katmandu, 46, kirkpatrickat, 65-66
Kautilya, 13
Kawaguchi, 93
Khadrub, 8
Khagendra Narayan, 34
Kienlung, 82, 91
Kinloch (captain), 34
Kirkpatrick, 17, 45 ; at Tibet, 51 ; at Nepal, 65-66 ; on Nepal,
              74, 83
Knox (captain), 46
Kublai khan, 8, 77
Kuch Behar, 32, 58

L

Ladak, 6
Lama, 6, 57
Lamaism, 6
Lamb, Alstair, 83
Laufer, Berth hold, 14

Lhasa, red hill of, 6 ; first European at 14 ; Capuchin's
       mission at, 14, 20 ; merchandise at, 21 ; trade route
       to China, 23, 48, 53 ; Manning in, 55, 56 ; Chinese
       inhabitants in 58, 59, 61 ; authorities unwilling to
       accept interference of the Chinese, 110
Lobsong kalsang, 78
Logan, James, 33
London, 27, 36, 48, 83
Lopon Rimpoche, 7

M

Macao, 29
Macartney, embassy of, 83, 84
Macaulay, Colman, 12

ERRATA

Page	line	incorrect	correct
10	11	latter	later
17	15	cconsumption	consumption
17	20	prospetive	prospective
20	24	Kashmiries	Kashmiris
21	24	empire	empire'
21	30	trade	trade.
30	2	were	was
34	28	intereference	interference
39	25	Arcnives	Archives
43	13	Nepal	Nepal,
45	6	end	end'
66	24	later on	later on.
73	8	Mongal	Mongol
73	23	statue	stated
92	29	relations	relation
92	37	thet	that